SALLY'S
COOKIE ADDICTION

Irresistible Cookies, Bars, Shortbread, and More
from the Creator of Sally's Baking Addiction

SALLY McKENNEY

Race Point
PUBLISHING

Brimming with creative inspiration, how-to projects, and useful information to enrich your everyday life, Quarto Knows is a favorite destination for those pursuing their interests and passions. Visit our site and dig deeper with our books into your area of interest: Quarto Creates, Quarto Cooks, Quarto Homes, Quarto Lives, Quarto Drives, Quarto Explores, Quarto Gifts, or Quarto Kids.

First published in 2017 by Race Point Publishing, an imprint of The Quarto Group, 142 West 36th Street, 4th Floor, New York, NY 10018, USA
T (212) 779-4972 F (212) 779-6058 **www.QuartoKnows.com**

Race Point Publishing titles are also available at discount for retail, wholesale, promotional, and bulk purchase. For details, contact the Special Sales Manager by email at specialsales@quarto.com or by mail at The Quarto Group, Attn: Special Sales Manager, 401 Second Avenue North, Suite 310, Minneapolis, MN 55401, USA.

10 9 8 7 6 5 4 3 2 1

ISBN: 978-1-63106-307-7

Library of Congress Cataloging-in-Publication Data

Names: McKenney, Sally, author.
Title: Sally's cookie addiction : irresistible cookies, cookie bars,
   shortbread, and more from the creator of Sally's baking addiction / Sally
   McKenney.
Description: New York, NY, USA : Race Point Publishing, an imprint of the
   Quarto Group, 2017. | Includes index.
Identifiers: LCCN 2017018781 | ISBN 9781631063077 (hardcover)
Subjects: LCSH: Cookies. | LCGFT: Cookbooks.
Classification: LCC TX772 .M364 2017 | DDC 641.86/54--dc23 LC record available at https://lccn.loc.gov/2017018781

Editorial Director: Jeannine Dillon
Creative Director: Merideth Harte
Project Editor: Erin Canning
Cover Design: Merideth Harte
Interior Design: Jacqui Caulton

Printed in China

To My Supportive, Encouraging,
and Cookie-Loving Family.

Contents

Family Favorites

All About Oats

Happy Holidays

Shortbread and Slice-and-Bakes Galore

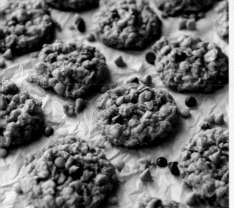

INTRODUCTION

◇◇

There's a time and a place for a fresh batch of cookies and that place is your kitchen and the time is *always*. Cookies not only taste wonderful, but they bring loved ones together—more than any other baked good coming out of our ovens. And isn't that what baking is all about?

Baking has always been a family affair for me, especially around the holidays when we finally put our hectic lives on pause and come together to celebrate. The chaos and stress of real life seems to disappear as we spend hours together in the kitchen decorating sugar cookies and arranging warm cookies on cooling racks. We box up fresh-baked cookies for gift-giving and cookie exchanges, but we always keep one tray aside for indulging ourselves—a little reward for our hard work.

While baking cookies in my own kitchen, I always think back to those pristine memories of baking with my family and loved ones. Even though it may be a random Tuesday and there's no holiday in sight, I'm still passionate about crafting that perfect handheld comfort food—a treat that brings a smile to anyone who takes a bite.

The immaculate combination of sugar and butter is what makes a cookie so irresistible, but the secret ingredient that makes cookies unbelievably addicting is love. That may sound corny (hi, have we met?), but a cookie that someone has spent hours mixing, rolling, and baking just for you can't help but taste incredible . . . even if you've accidentally burned the bottom (guilty).

In the past six years since I launched *Sally's Baking Addiction*, I've witnessed firsthand the undeniable allure of the cookie. They're the most popular category of recipe on my blog and my most requested recipes. I think it's because they're relatively easy and approachable. Most cookies don't require a ton of special equipment, and if you can follow a recipe, you can make a pretty fabulous batch of snickerdoodles that taste even better than the ones you had growing up (page 18!). They're also an easy treat to share, which is part of the reason they bring people together, especially kids. If you want to get a group of kids to come to the table, put a plate of cookies out. Portable and perfect for gifting, cookies can be made in large batches for bake sales, parties, or for your new neighbor down the street or that cousin who just had a baby. I've never met anyone who doesn't appreciate a box of fresh-baked homemade cookies. Have you?

Which brings me to why I created this cookbook. The heart of it is homemade, a wide range of cookies, all baked from scratch with love, confidence, and passion. You'll find classic cookies, filled cookies, flavored cookies, sugar cookies, thin cookies, thick cookies, soft cookies, and crunchy cookies. And that's just another reason to fall in love with the cookie: the word can be used on an infinite number of sweet creations, from cookie cups and cookie bars to sandwich cookies. There is no hard-and-fast definition as to what a cookie needs to be (well, except delicious).

This book is divided into eight chapters, with recipes grouped together based on their flavors, ingredients, or time of year. The first chapter is all about Family Favorites. This is where you'll find the recipes that generate the most buzz, such as chocolate chip cookies and sugar cookies.

I invite you to join me in the kitchen, wander through this book, and find your favorites to bake. Be sure to read the following pages in this section for general, invaluable information, and read each recipe two or three times before you start baking. The *Sally Says* and Make-Ahead tips sprinkled throughout the recipes are also helpful. The few minutes spent preparing could save you from a ruined batch!

Create, taste, enjoy, and most of all—share.

—Sally

Key Ingredients

Brown sugar: Brown sugar is granulated sugar with a touch of molasses added, making it super soft and moist. Dark brown sugar has a touch more molasses, but the two can be used interchangeably in any of my recipes. However, I list my preferred type in the recipe where applicable. Whichever you use, make sure you pack it into the measuring cup.

Butter: All of the recipes in this cookbook were tested with unsalted butter. If you substitute salted butter instead, make sure you reduce the salt used in the recipe by ¼ teaspoon per ½ cup (¼ stick, or 60 g) of butter. I do not recommend substituting margarine in these cookie recipes.

Chocolate: Some of the recipes in this book call for a specific number of ounces of pure chocolate. This type of chocolate is the best for melting. There are several different kinds of chocolate on the market: unsweetened, semi-sweet, bittersweet, white, etc. The recipes specify which is best. This type of chocolate is typically sold in bar form, usually 4 ounces (113 g) each. I prefer Ghirardelli, Baker's, or Lindt brands.

Chocolate chips: When I refer to chocolate chips or white chocolate chips in this book, I mean packaged chocolate chips, such as those by Nestlé® Toll House®. Chocolate chips are formulated so that they do not lose their shape when exposed to high oven heat. Don't use them unless the recipe specifically calls for them.

Cream cheese: Make sure you use full-fat blocks of cream cheese. Do not use cream cheese spread (in the tubs) for recipes in this book.

Cream of tartar: Cream of tartar acts as an acid in cookie baking, but it can also be used to stabilize egg whites, such as in Fairy Meringues (page 120). It's a crucial ingredient for the recipe's chemistry, so don't skip it. Science is tasty, isn't it?

Cocoa powder: There are two types of cocoa powder used in baking: natural and Dutch-processed. Most supermarkets in the United States sell natural, while Dutch-processed is more common in Europe. The difference between the two, from a baking standpoint, is huge. Dutch-processed cocoa is neutral, while natural cocoa is an acid. Dutching cocoa powder gives it a more mellow flavor compared to the natural style. Do not use the two interchangeably in recipes unless the recipe instructs that either is appropriate.

Confectioners' sugar: Also known as powdered sugar or icing sugar. Confectioners' sugar is ultra-fine sugar with a smooth and powdery consistency. I prefer to use it as the sweetener in buttery-soft cookies such as the shortbread recipes (page 85).

Cornstarch: Often sold as "corn flour" outside of the United States. I like to use a touch of cornstarch to soften some cookie doughs.

Eggs: All of the recipes in this book calling for eggs were tested with large eggs. Make sure your eggs are at room temperature if the recipe calls for room temperature or uses melted butter. It's imperative that all ingredients in cookie recipes are at a similar temperature (see page 11, tip #4). A few recipes call for an extra egg yolk. This extra yolk provides fat, moisture, flavor, and tenderness when I feel the dough needs it. Don't skip it!

Granulated sugar: Granulated sugar is your everyday, regular white sugar.

Meringue powder: Meringue powder is my go-to for making Traditional Royal Icing (page 15). It's made primarily from dried egg whites and provides stability to the icing, ensuring it holds its shape and finishes with a stiff texture.

Molasses: I prefer using unsulphured molasses in my baking. Sulphured molasses has been treated with sulphur dioxide and can leave a pronounced chemical aftertaste. For the most robust flavor, choose an unsulphured molasses labeled as "dark" as opposed to sulphured molasses labeled "light" or "mild."

Peanut butter: All of the recipes in this cookbook calling for peanut butter were tested with Jif® or Skippy® brand. I advise against using homemade or natural and oily peanut butters because the thinner texture will act completely different in a cookie recipe.

Oats: There are many types of oats on the market, but the only type you will need for the recipes in this cookbook are old-fashioned whole rolled oats. They're thicker and less powdery than the thinner-cut quick and instant oats.

Sprinkles: There's a whole section dedicated to sprinkles (obviously), so flip to page 107 for more detail!

Vanilla extract: When buying vanilla extract make sure that it's labeled "pure." Don't reach for a bottle labeled "imitation," as it isn't nearly as potent and is made with synthetic vanilla that leaves a bitter aftertaste.

Sally Says

As with any recipe, if you vary ingredients or make substitutions, the results will likely not be the same.

Kitchen Essentials

Here are all of the tools you'll need to get baking the recipes in this book. Make sure you thoroughly read the recipes before starting so you know what is required or what tool limitations you may have.

- Baking pans (9 × 13-inch, or 23 × 33 cm; two 24-count mini-muffin pans; and 12-inch, or 30 cm, pizza pan)
- Baking sheets (2 or 3 large ones)
- Cookie cutters (including 1-inch, or 2.5 cm, and 2-inch, or 5 cm, round cookie cutters)
- Cookie scoops (No. 60 scoop, or 1 tablespoon; No. 40, or 1½ tablespoons—I like OXO's medium cookie scoop; No. 30, or 2 tablespoons; and No. 16, or ¼ cup)
- Cooling racks (2 or 3 of them)
- Decorating tips (various sizes)
- Electric mixer (handheld or stand mixer fitted with a paddle attachment)
- Food processor
- Heatproof bowls (small, medium, and large)
- Kitchen scale
- Measuring cups

- Measuring spoons
- Mixing bowls (small, medium, and large)
- Oven thermometer
- Parchment paper
- Pastry brush
- Pastry cutter
- Rolling pin
- Rubber spatulas
- Ruler
- Silicone baking mats (2 or 3 of them; see page 10, tip #9)
- Skillets (small light-colored one and 10-inch, or 25 cm, oven-safe)
- Whisk
- Wooden spoons
- Zest grater (I use a hand grater)

Sally's Top 10 Cookie-Making Tips

From my kitchen to yours, here are my top 10 cookie-baking tips. Make your next batch the BEST batch!

1. **Chill out!** My number one tip is to chill your cookie dough. Chilling the dough solidifies the fat, which will result in puffier, sturdier, and thicker cookies. Also, the flavors have a chance to marry after a few hours in the refrigerator. After you chill the cookie dough, it will probably be quite hard. Let it sit out on the counter for 10 to 30 minutes so it's scoopable.

2. **Butter is better.** Make sure your butter is at the proper temperature. The majority of recipes in this cookbook call for room-temperature butter. This means that the butter is pliable enough that your finger can leave a mark in it, without being too soft or greasy. For best results, set the butter out 1 hour prior to starting. To speed up the process, slice the butter into tablespoon (15 g) slices and place on a plate. It will soften quicker than if it were kept whole.

3. **Turn up the heat!** Buy an oven thermometer. They're inexpensive and will save you from many ruined baked goods. An oven's temperature can be off by as much as 50°F, or 10°C, proving it's not as reliable as you thought. An oven's internal thermometer measures the temperature depending on where it's located, which could be in the front, side, or back of the box. But an oven thermometer placed inside can tell you what the actual temperature is in the center of the oven, where you bake cookies.

4. **Switch it up!** Rotate your baking pans. I usually only bake one batch of cookies at a time, because I find overcrowding the oven can alter their texture. But when I'm crunched for time, I bake two batches at once. Rotating the pans from top to bottom halfway through baking ensures each tray will bake evenly. Ovens have hot spots!

5. **Leave breathing room.** Don't overcrowd the baking sheets. I typically only bake 8 or 9 cookies per baking sheet, unless otherwise noted in the recipe. Depending on the size of the cookies, I find that baking 12 cookies at a time overcrowds the pan and each cookie doesn't have enough room to spread and cook properly.

6. **Stick to the middle ground.** I always use the middle rack. You get the best possible results when the oven only concentrates on one batch in the very center.

7. **Go with your gut.** The one time I'll tell you to NOT follow a recipe is right here: forget the listed bake time. There, I said it. Instead, use the bake times as a guide. All ovens are different. When I moved into my new home, I found that my trusted cookie recipes took a minute or two longer than normal in my new oven. And it's okay! Look at the cookies to determine their doneness. The cookies are ready when the edges are set and lightly browned. The top center can look a little underbaked because the cookies will continue to cook for a few minutes while cooling.

8. **Follow the 5-minute rule.** Allow the cookies to cool on a wire rack. Most recipes in this cookbook will instruct you to let the cookies cool for 5 minutes on the baking sheet. This is so they can continue setting. After that, immediately transfer them to a wire rack so the bottoms of the cookies get some much-needed air.

9. **Respect the mat!** Bake your cookies on a silicone baking mat. These mats are my favorite cookie-baking tool! Coating your baking sheet with nonstick spray or butter creates an overly greasy foundation, causing the cookies to spread. I always recommend a silicone baking mat because they grip onto the bottom of your cookie dough, preventing the cookies from spreading too much. These mats also promote even browning.

10. **Carbs rule.** Store your cookies with a slice of bread. This is a weird tip, for sure! I store my cookies in a cookie jar, airtight plastic container, or a large zip-top bag. And I always keep a slice of bread on top of the cookies. This slice of bread will let out its moisture into the cookies, keeping them extra soft and fresh. The bread turns hard after a few days because all of its moisture has been transferred to your now deliciously soft cookies!

How to Prevent Excess Spreading

In other words, how to prevent the puddle problem. You know what I'm talking about. You put your cookies in the oven expecting them to spread a little bit only to discover cookie puddles, all over your baking sheet. Here are a few tips that will help you avoid this cookie catastrophe.

Be exact. Measure ingredients properly. Sounds like a no-brainer, right? Well, measuring is something we often rush, when, in fact, it's the most important part of following a recipe. One common mistake is measuring flour. Make sure you spoon and level it—spoon flour into the measuring cup and level it off with a knife. **Do not pack the flour down.** Another common mistake is using the wrong size egg. Make sure you use large eggs, not extra-large, for the recipes in this cookbook.

No substitutions. Speaking of ingredients, make sure not to deviate from the original recipe. I get a lot of questions about cookies spreading, and when I discuss with the reader what happened, it's often because they substituted an ingredient. Follow the recipe as written for best results.

Exasperation with expiration! Are your leavening agents fresh? Baking powder and baking soda quickly lose their potency. I like to replace mine after just 3 months, as I find their strength dwindling not much longer after that!

Room temperature, please. Unless otherwise noted, room temperature ingredients are imperative. Creaming room temperature butter with sugar, a common step in most cookie recipes, incorporates air into the cookie dough. If the butter is too cool, it's impossible to whip in enough air, thus resulting in flat cookies. Likewise, always make sure your eggs are room temperature, too.

Don't go crazy. It is possible to beat TOO much air into your cookie dough. This results in a puffy cookie that will end up collapsing as it cools. Make sure you follow the recipe and cream the butter and sugar for however long the recipe states, usually 1 to 2 minutes.

Cold pays off. Chill your cookie dough. The most common culprit behind the cookie-puddle problem is starting with warm and sticky dough. Chilling cookie dough is required for the majority of the recipes in this cookbook. This crucial step solidifies the fat in the dough, resulting in puffier, sturdier, and thicker cookies.

Hot sheets are a no-no. Never place cookie dough on a hot baking sheet. If you're baking a lot of cookies at a time, invest in a couple extra baking sheets so you'll always have a room-temperature sheet on hand.

Make-Ahead Tips and Freezing Instructions

No one is perfect, so that's why I provide make-ahead and freezing instructions for every single cookie recipe in this book. Why take a chance on not having perfect cookies when you need them? Whether you have sudden unexpected guests in need of a sweet treat or you have to cook a whole meal for the holiday and want to make some things in advance, this is the section for you!

Drop Cookies
For most drop cookies (the ones you roll or scoop into balls), such as chocolate chip cookies and oatmeal cookies, the make-ahead and freezing instructions are exactly the same and listed here.

Making dough ahead of time: Prepare the cookie dough as directed in the recipe. Cover the bowl with plastic wrap or aluminum foil and chill the dough in the refrigerator for up to 4 days. Allow the dough to come to room temperature then continue with rolling and shaping the cookies as directed in the recipe.

Freezing cookie dough: Wrap up the dough tightly in plastic wrap and place into a zip-top bag. Label the bag with the month and the recipe name. Labeling helps you determine the freshness and which recipe it is (no cookie left behind)! Place the bag in the freezer. Cookie dough freezes well for up to 3 months, unless otherwise noted in the recipe. When it's time to bake the cookies, remove the dough from the freezer and allow to thaw overnight in the refrigerator. If the cookie dough is still rock-hard the next morning, let it sit out at room temperature for a couple hours before rolling and baking.

Freezing cookie dough balls: You can also freeze the cookie dough after you've rolled it into balls, which is what I usually do. After the cookie dough has chilled in the refrigerator (if the recipe requires chilling), roll or scoop the cookie dough into balls as instructed in the recipe. Then, chill the dough balls for 1 hour to ensure they are solid. (This prevents them from sticking together in the freezer.) Place the solid, chilled cookie dough balls into a zip-top bag that you've labeled, as I mention in "freezing cookie dough." Place the bag in the freezer. Cookie dough balls freeze well for up to 3 months. When it's time to bake the cookies, remove the dough balls from the freezer. You can either allow them to thaw in the refrigerator and bake as directed in the recipe OR bake while frozen. If baking the frozen dough balls, add 1 to 2 minutes to the bake time.

Note: If the cookies are rolled in sprinkles or cinnamon sugar such as Brown Butter Snickerdoodles (page 18) or Sugar Cookie Sparkles (page 110), freeze the cookie dough balls **without the topping**. When you are ready to bake, remove the balls from freezer, let them sit for 30 minutes, preheat the oven, and then roll them into the topping. No need to bake for an extra minute or two since the cookies have defrosted a little.

Freezing baked cookies: Most cookies that have already been baked freeze well for up to 3 months unless otherwise noted in the recipe. Layer the cookies between parchment paper in a freezer-safe container or simply pile them into a zip-top bag. Thaw baked cookies overnight in the refrigerator and bring to room temperature, if desired, before serving.

Frosting and Icing

Vanilla Frosting

Creamy and soft, this basic vanilla frosting can be used on everything from cookies to cookie bars and cups and other treats.

PREP TIME: 5 minutes   **TOTAL TIME:** 5 minutes   **YIELD:** 1½ cups

½ cup (1 stick, or 120 g) unsalted butter, softened to room temperature
1¾ cups (210 g) confectioners' sugar
2 tablespoons (30 ml) heavy cream or milk
1¼ teaspoons pure vanilla extract
pinch salt (optional)

1. In a large bowl, using a handheld mixer or a stand mixer fitted with a paddle or whisk attachment, beat the butter on medium-high speed until smooth, about 1 minute. Add the confectioners' sugar, cream, and vanilla extract, and beat on low speed for 20 seconds, then increase to high speed until combined, about 1 minute.

2. Taste and add a pinch of salt, if desired.

Glaze Icing

If royal icing isn't your thing, try this easy glaze icing instead. I usually use an empty squeeze bottle for decorating cookies when working with this glaze icing. It's not as stable as royal icing, but when applied in a thin layer, it will dry within 24 hours.

PREP TIME: 5 minutes   **TOTAL TIME:** 5 minutes   **YIELD:** 1 cup

1½ cups (180 g) confectioners' sugar, sifted, plus more if needed
½ teaspoon pure vanilla extract
1 teaspoon light corn syrup
2 to 2½ tablespoons (30 to 38 ml) room temperature water
pinch salt (optional)

1. Whisk the confectioners' sugar, vanilla extract, corn syrup, and 2 tablespoons (30 ml) of water in a medium bowl until combined. The icing will be quite thick. Using the whisk, drizzle a little of the icing back into the bowl. If it's the right consistency, the ribbon of icing will hold for a couple seconds then disappear and smooth out into the icing. If the icing is too thick to pipe onto cookies, add ½ tablespoon (8 ml) of water. If it's too thin, add 2 tablespoons (30 ml) of confectioners' sugar.

2. Taste and add a pinch of salt, if desired.

Traditional Royal Icing

This is, hands down, my favorite icing for decorating sugar cookies! It dries within a couple hours. For tips, see Royal Icing 101 below.

PREP TIME: 10 minutes   **TOTAL TIME:** 10 minutes   **YIELD:** 2½ cups

4 cups (480 g) confectioners' sugar, sifted, plus more if needed
3 tablespoons (30 g) meringue powder
6 to 7 tablespoons (90 to 105 ml) room temperature water

In a large bowl, using a handheld mixer or a stand mixer fitted with a whisk attachment, beat all of the ingredients together on high speed for a 5 full minutes. When lifting the whisk out of the bowl, the icing should drizzle down and smooth out within 10 seconds. If it's too thick, add a teaspoon or 2 of water, as needed. If it's too thin, add 1 or 2 tablespoons (7.5 or 15 ml) of sifted confectioners' sugar.

ROYAL ICING 101

- The meringue powder is what allows this royal icing to dry hard, which is what makes royal icing so versatile and convenient. This trait is particularly handy when you're stacking, shipping, or gifting sugar cookies.

- This royal icing is perfect for outlining designs and for flooding on top of cookies.

- If you're working with only a little royal icing at a time, make sure you place a moist paper towel on top of the bowl of icing, so it does not dry out as you work.

- Air bubbles? Icing that is too thin can end up with air bubbles and an uneven texture. It's best to keep the icing on the thick side. See the instructions in the recipe for the consistency you should work toward.

- If it's a super humid day, you may need a tablespoon or 2 (15 or 30 ml) less water. Alternatively, if it's a super dry day, you may need up to 8 or 9 tablespoons (120 or 135 ml) of room temperature water.

- My favorite piping tips include Wilton® #5 Round Decorating Tip and Wilton® #1 Round Decorating Tip.

- I find gel food coloring best when tinting royal icing. Add only 1 small drop at a time until you reach your desired shade.

Family Favorites

The entire book is filled with traditional recipes with a few unique variations and flavors. This particular chapter, however, focuses on family favorites that we can't live without. We're talking chocolate chip cookies, snickerdoodles, and sugar cookies. Like a red lipstick or little black dress, these classics will never go out of style. These are the cookies we grew up on, bake with our kids, and sell at bake sales.

The recipes filling the following pages are what I learned to bake first. I distinctly remember lining up chocolate chip cookies on the counter with my mama to cool. Next came the snickerdoodles and, finally, the sugar cookies. There's a reason these cookies are forever favorites: they're simple, delicious, and always made with love.

With family favorites like these, it's nearly impossible not to devour every single page. But before you get started, let me warn you that the last recipe in this chapter isn't really for HUMANS to devour. . . .

Brown Butter Snickerdoodles

If you aren't already madly in love with the cinnamon sugar delights we all know as snickerdoodles, you will be after trying this version. Brown butter, with its nutty and toasty flavor, completely changes everything!

PREP TIME: 15 minutes   **TOTAL TIME:** 1 hour   **YIELD:** 36 to 40 cookies

1 cup (2 sticks, or 240 g) butter, cut into 16 tablespoons

2¼ cups (270 g) all-purpose flour

1 teaspoon cream of tartar

1 teaspoon baking soda

½ teaspoon salt

¾ cup (170 g) packed light brown sugar

1¼ cups (250 g) granulated sugar, divided

1 large egg, room temperature

1 tablespoon (15 ml) milk

1½ teaspoons pure vanilla extract

2 teaspoons ground cinnamon

MAKE-AHEAD TIP

See page 12.

1. Brown the butter: Have a large heatproof bowl handy. Place butter in a light-colored skillet over medium heat. (The light color of the skillet makes it easier to determine when the butter begins browning.) Whisking constantly, melt the butter. The butter will begin to foam. After 5 to 8 minutes, the butter will begin browning—you'll notice lightly browned specks starting to form at the bottom of the pan (see photo, left), and there will be a nutty aroma. Once browned, remove from the heat immediately to stop the browning process, and pour into the heatproof bowl. Allow the butter to cool for 5 minutes.

2. Meanwhile, whisk the flour, cream of tartar, baking soda, and salt together in a medium bowl. Set aside.

3. Add the brown sugar and ¾ cup (150 g) of the granulated sugar to the browned butter. Using a handheld mixer or a stand mixer fitted with a paddle attachment, beat together on medium-high speed until relatively combined, about 1 minute. Beat in the egg, milk, and vanilla extract until combined.

4. Pour the dry ingredients into the wet ingredients and begin beating together on low speed, slowly working up to high speed until everything is combined. The dough will be thick and a little greasy.

5. Mix the remaining ½ cup (100 g) granulated sugar and the cinnamon together in a small bowl.

6. Roll balls of dough, about 1 tablespoon per cookie, then roll each in the cinnamon sugar mixture. Do not discard remaining cinnamon sugar mixture. Place the dough balls tightly together on a lined baking sheet (or a couple of large plates). Loosely cover the dough balls with plastic wrap and place in the refrigerator to chill for 30 minutes (and up to 4 days).

7. Preheat oven to 350°F (180°C). Line a second baking sheet with parchment paper or a silicone baking mat.

8. Place chilled dough balls onto the baking sheets, also using the prepared sheet from step 7, about 3 inches (7.5 cm) apart. Sprinkle each with any extra cinnamon sugar. Bake for 11 minutes, or until lightly browned on the sides. Remove from the oven and allow to cool on the baking sheets for 5 minutes, then transfer to a wire rack to cool completely.

9. Cookies will stay fresh in an airtight container at room temperature for up to 1 week.

White Chocolate Macadamia Nut Cookies

A classic if there ever was one. These super-soft, buttery cookies are filled to the brim with sweet white chocolate chips and salty macadamia nuts. Enjoy them while you can because they disappear quickly!

PREP TIME: 30 minutes   **TOTAL TIME:** 3 hours   **YIELD:** 24 cookies

2 cups (240 g) all-purpose flour

1 teaspoon baking soda

1 teaspoon cornstarch

½ teaspoon salt

¾ cup (1½ sticks, or 180 g) unsalted butter, softened to room temperature

¾ cup (170 g) packed brown sugar

¼ cup (50 g) granulated sugar

1 large egg, room temperature

2 teaspoons pure vanilla extract

¾ cup (125 g) white chocolate chips

¾ cup (100 g) chopped salted macadamia nuts

MAKE-AHEAD TIP

See page 12.

Sally Says

Why cornstarch? As you learned in Key Ingredients on page 8, a teeny amount makes your cookies even softer. Trust me on this!

1. Whisk the flour, baking soda, cornstarch, and salt together in a medium bowl. Set aside.

2. In a large bowl, using a handheld mixer or a stand mixer fitted with a paddle attachment, beat the butter on medium-high speed until smooth, about 1 minute. Add the brown sugar and granulated sugar, and beat on medium-high speed until creamed, about 2 minutes. Add the egg and vanilla extract, then beat on high speed until combined, about 1 minute. Scrape down the sides and up the bottom of the bowl, and beat again as needed to combine.

3. Add the dry ingredients to the wet ingredients and mix on low speed until combined. With the mixer running on low speed, add the white chocolate chips and macadamia nuts. The dough will be thick. Cover and chill the dough in the refrigerator for at least 2 hours (and up to 4 days). If chilling for longer than 3 hours, allow it to sit at room temperature for at least 30 minutes before rolling and baking because the dough will be quite hard.

4. Preheat oven to 350°F (180°C). Line baking sheets with parchment paper or silicone baking mats. Set aside.

5. Roll balls of dough, about 1½ tablespoons of dough per cookie, and place 3 inches (7.5 cm) apart on the baking sheets. Bake for 11 to 12 minutes, or until lightly browned on the sides. The centers will look very soft.

6. Remove from the oven and allow to cool on the baking sheets for 5 minutes before transferring to a wire rack to cool completely.

7. Cookies will stay fresh in an airtight container at room temperature for up to 1 week.

1 Cookie Dough, 3 Different Cookies

One cookie dough with infinite possibilities! Here you'll use the recipe for my favorite Soft & Chewy Chocolate Chip Cookies (page 25), but you'll replace the chocolate chips with one of three incredible combinations of add-ins presented below.

PREP TIME: 15 minutes   **TOTAL TIME:** 2 hours, 50 minutes   **YIELD:** 22 to 24 cookies

Base Cookie Dough

2¼ cups (270 g) all-purpose flour
1½ teaspoons cornstarch
1 teaspoon baking soda
½ teaspoon salt
¾ cup (1½ sticks, or 180 g) unsalted butter, melted and slightly cooled
¾ cup (170 g) packed light brown sugar
½ cup (50 g) granulated sugar
1 large egg plus 1 egg yolk, both at room temperature
2 teaspoons pure vanilla extract

Add-Ins (choose 1 combination)

- **Cranberry Orange White Chocolate Chip:** 1 cup (170 g) white chocolate chips plus ¾ cup (115 g) dried cranberries plus zest of 1 orange.
- **Sweet and Salty M&M's® Combo:** 1 cup (45 g) pretzel pieces plus ¾ cup (126 g) mini M&M's® plus sprinkle of sea salt (add the sea salt to warm cookies when they come out of the oven).
- **Cinnamon Chocolate Pecan:** 1 teaspoon ground cinnamon plus 1 cup (180 g) semi-sweet chocolate chips plus ¾ cup (80 g) chopped pecans.

1. Whisk the flour, cornstarch, baking soda, and salt together in a medium bowl. Set aside.

2. In a large bowl, whisk the butter, brown sugar, and granulated sugar together until combined and no brown sugar lumps remain. Whisk in the egg and egg yolk, then whisk in the vanilla until combined.

3. Add the dry ingredients to the wet ingredients and stir with a rubber spatula or wooden spoon until the cookie dough comes together. Stir in the desired add-ins. The dough will be very soft. Cover and chill the dough in the refrigerator for at least 2 hours (and up to 4 days). If chilling for longer than 3 hours, allow it to sit at room temperature for at least 30 minutes before rolling and baking because the dough will be quite hard.

4. Preheat oven to 325°F (170°C). Line baking sheets with parchment paper or silicone baking mats. Set aside.

5. Roll balls of dough, 2 scant tablespoons of dough per cookie, and arrange 3 inches (7.5 cm) apart on the baking sheets. Bake for 12 to 13 minutes, or until lightly browned on the sides. The centers will look soft.

6. Remove from the oven and allow to cool on the baking sheets for 5 minutes before transferring to a wire rack to cool completely.

7. Cookies will stay fresh in an airtight container at room temperature for up to 1 week.

MAKE-AHEAD TIP

See page 12.

Soft & Chewy Chocolate Chip Cookies

Do you prefer your chocolate chip cookies extra soft or crispy around the edges? It's been a long-running debate for years in the cookie world, and my readers seem split on the issue. Crispy edges are good, but so is melt-in-your-mouth softness. So which is better? The answer is BOTH. The recipe below is for those of you who prefer soft-baked chocolate chip cookies, and it is one of the most beloved on my website. The secret to their soft and chewy texture is an extra egg yolk, more brown sugar than white, melted butter, and a slightly lower oven temperature. Cornstarch keeps them extra soft, and you already know how important it is to chill that dough, people!

PREP TIME: 15 minutes **TOTAL TIME:** 2 hours 50 minutes **YIELD:** 24 to 30 cookies

2¼ cups (270 g) all-purpose flour

1½ teaspoons cornstarch

1 teaspoon baking soda

½ teaspoon salt

¾ cup (1½ sticks, or 180 g) unsalted butter, melted and slightly cooled

¾ cup (170 g) packed light brown sugar

½ cup (50 g) granulated sugar

1 large egg plus 1 egg yolk, both at room temperature

2 teaspoons pure vanilla extract

1⅓ cups (240 g) semi-sweet chocolate chips

MAKE-AHEAD TIP

See page 12.

SALLY SAYS

This is definitely my favorite base cookie dough for a variety of exciting flavors. I use it so much in fact that I have it memorized! You can personalize this chocolate chip cookie dough base with your own favorite add-in flavors like I did on page 22.

1. Whisk the flour, cornstarch, baking soda, and salt together in a medium bowl. Set aside.

2. In a large bowl, whisk the butter, brown sugar, and granulated sugar together until combined and no brown sugar lumps remain. Whisk in the egg and egg yolk, then whisk in the vanilla extract until combined.

3. Add the dry ingredients to the wet ingredients and stir with a rubber spatula or wooden spoon until the cookie dough comes together. Stir in the chocolate chips. The dough will be very soft and even a little wet. Cover and chill the dough in the refrigerator for at least 2 hours (and up to 4 days). If chilling for longer than 3 hours, allow it to sit at room temperature for at least 30 minutes before rolling and baking because the dough will be quite hard.

4. Preheat oven to 325°F (170°C). Line baking sheets with parchment paper or silicone baking mats. Set aside.

5. Roll balls of dough, 2 scant tablespoons of dough per cookie, and place 3 inches (7.5 cm) apart on the baking sheets. Bake for 12 to 13 minutes, or until lightly browned on the sides. The centers will look soft.

6. Remove from the oven and allow to cool on the baking sheets for 5 minutes before transferring to a wire rack to cool completely.

7. Cookies will stay fresh in an airtight container at room temperature for up to 1 week.

CRISPY-EDGED CHOCOLATE CHIP COOKIES

If you're a crispy-edge cookie lover, don't feel left out! This recipe was formulated and perfected just for this cookbook, and I haven't shared it on my blog before. It took some work—and even more butter—to land upon a chocolate chip cookie that has both super-crisp edges AND doesn't overspread in the oven. The secret? More white sugar than brown sugar, a little milk, and a longer bake time. Time in the refrigerator helps firm up the dough so the cookies don't overspread on your baking sheets. Don't miss this one if you love a bit of crisp in your chocolate chip cookie!

PREP TIME: 15 minutes   **TOTAL TIME:** 1 hour 15 minutes   **YIELD:** 24 to 30 cookies

2 cups plus 2 tablespoons (255 g) all-purpose flour
1 teaspoon baking soda
½ teaspoon salt
¾ cup (1½ sticks, or 180 g) unsalted butter, softened to room temperature
1 cup (200 g) granulated sugar
⅓ cup (75 g) packed brown sugar
1 large egg, room temperature
2 teaspoons pure vanilla extract
1 tablespoon (15 ml) milk
2 cups (360 g) semi-sweet chocolate chips

MAKE-AHEAD TIP

See page 12.

SALLY SAYS

Why an extra 2 tablespoons (30 ml) of flour? I found the cookies spread too much with only 2 cups (240 g), so don't leave out those extra tablespoons. They help soak up some moisture.

1. Whisk the flour, baking soda, and salt together in a medium bowl. Set aside.

2. In a large bowl, using a handheld mixer or a stand mixer fitted with a paddle attachment, beat the butter on medium-high speed until smooth, about 1 minute. Add the granulated sugar and brown sugar, and beat on medium-high speed until creamed, about 2 minutes. Add the egg and vanilla extract, then beat on high speed until combined, about 1 minute. Scrape down the sides and up the bottom of the bowl and beat again as needed to combine.

3. Add the dry ingredients to the wet ingredients and mix on low speed until combined. With the mixer running on low speed, add the milk and chocolate chips. The dough will be soft and thick. Cover and chill the dough in the refrigerator for at least 30 minutes (and up to 4 days). If chilling for longer than 3 hours, allow it to sit at room temperature for at least 30 minutes before rolling and baking because the dough will be quite hard.

4. Preheat oven to 350°F (180°C). Line baking sheets with parchment paper or silicone baking mats. Set aside.

5. Roll balls of dough, about 1½ tablespoons of dough per cookie, and place 3 inches (7.5 cm) apart on the baking sheets. Bake for 14 to 16 minutes, or until lightly browned on the sides and tops.

6. Remove from the oven and allow to cool on the baking sheets for 5 minutes before transferring to a wire rack to cool completely.

7. Cookies will stay fresh in an airtight container at room temperature for up to 1 week.

Super-Chewy Chocolate Chip Cookie Bars

Also known as "spread-and-bake" chocolate chip cookies, these couldn't be easier! Check out my sugar cookie version, Soft-Baked Sugar Cookie Bars (page 112).

PREP TIME: 15 minutes   **TOTAL TIME:** 3 hours   **YIELD:** 24 bars

2¾ cups (330 g) all-purpose flour

1 teaspoon cornstarch

1 teaspoon baking soda

¾ teaspoon salt

¾ cup (1½ sticks, or 180 g) unsalted butter, softened to room temperature

2 cups (450 g) packed light brown sugar

2 large eggs plus 1 egg yolk, all at room temperature

2 teaspoons pure vanilla extract

1½ cups (270 g) semi-sweet chocolate chips

1 cup (120 g) chopped walnuts

Sally Says

Unlike regular chocolate chip cookies, I use all brown sugar in these bars for lots of flavor. And are you wondering about the cornstarch and extra egg yolk? See my explanation in the introduction to Soft & Chewy Chocolate Chip Cookies (page 25) as to why I use these ingredients.

1. Preheat oven to 350°F (180°C). Line a 9 × 13-inch (23 × 33 cm) baking pan with parchment paper, leaving enough overhang around the sides to easily lift the bars out. (I encourage parchment so that you can easily remove the baked dough as a whole and not cut it into bars while it's in the pan.)

2. Whisk the flour, cornstarch, baking soda, and salt together in a medium bowl. Set aside.

3. In a large bowl, whisk the butter and brown sugar together until combined. Whisk in the eggs and egg yolk, then whisk in the vanilla extract until combined.

4. Add the dry ingredients to the wet ingredients and stir with a rubber spatula or wooden spoon until the cookie dough comes together. Stir in the chocolate chips and walnuts. The dough will be soft, yet heavy.

5. Press the dough evenly into the prepared baking pan. Bake for 24 to 27 minutes, or until the edges and top are lightly browned.

6. Remove from the oven and allow to cool completely in the pan on a wire rack. Once cool, remove the baked dough from the pan by picking it up with the parchment paper on the sides. Cut into squares.

7. Bars will stay fresh in an airtight container at room temperature for up to 1 week.

MAKE-AHEAD TIP

Prepare the dough, following steps 2 through 4, then cover tightly and refrigerate for up to 3 days or freeze for up to 3 months. When ready to use, allow the dough to come to room temperature (if frozen, thaw in the refrigerator first), preheat the oven to 350°F (180°C), and continue with step 5. Baked bars can be frozen for up to 3 months; allow to thaw overnight in the refrigerator, then bring to room temperature before serving.

GIANT M&M'S® COOKIES

One of the largest cookies in this cookbook, these monster-size delights each consist of a whopping 4 tablespoons (¼ cup) of dough! There's no shortage of M&M's® either; every single soft-baked bite is packed with a rainbow of happiness.

PREP TIME: 30 minutes   **TOTAL TIME:** 3 hours   **YIELD:** 20 large cookies

3 cups (360 g) all-purpose flour
1 teaspoon baking soda
¾ teaspoon salt
1 cup (2 sticks, or 240 g) unsalted
  butter, softened to room temperature
1 cup (225 g) packed light brown sugar
1 cup (200 g) granulated sugar
2 large eggs, room temperature
1 tablespoon (15 ml) pure vanilla
  extract (yes, 1 full tablespoon!)
2¼ cups (378 g) M&M's® (mini, regular
  size, or a mix of both)

MAKE-AHEAD TIP

See page 12.

1. Whisk the flour, baking soda, and salt together in a medium bowl. Set aside.

2. In a large bowl, using a handheld mixer or a stand mixer fitted with a paddle attachment, beat the butter on medium-high speed until smooth, about 1 minute. Add the brown sugar and granulated sugar, and beat on medium-high speed until creamed, about 2 minutes. Add the eggs and vanilla extract, then beat on high speed until combined, about 1 minute. Scrape down the sides and up the bottom of the bowl and beat again as needed to combine.

3. Add the dry ingredients to the wet ingredients and mix on low speed until combined. With the mixer running on low speed, add the M&M's®. The dough will be soft and thick. Cover and chill the dough in the refrigerator for at least 2 hours (and up to 4 days). If chilling for longer than 3 hours, allow it to sit at room temperature for at least 30 minutes before rolling and baking because the dough will be quite hard.

4. Preheat oven to 350°F (180°C). Line baking sheets with parchment paper or silicone baking mats. Set aside.

5. Roll balls of dough, 4 tablespoons (¼ cup) of dough per cookie, and place 4 inches (10 cm) apart on the baking sheets. Bake for 15 to 17 minutes, or until lightly browned on the sides. The centers will still look soft.

6. Remove from the oven and allow to cool on the baking sheets for 5 minutes before transferring to a wire rack to cool completely.

7. Cookies will stay fresh in an airtight container at room temperature for up to 1 week.

Cookie Cutter Sugar Cookies

I had so much fun decorating these donut-shaped cookies! You can use any shape of cookie cutter you'd like; I'm just a sucker for frosted sprinkle donuts. (Who isn't?) This is my basic go-to sugar cookie dough. The trick is to roll out the cookie dough before chilling in the refrigerator. You'll chill the slabs of dough, then cut into shapes and bake. Remember, cold sugar cookie dough is much easier to work with and prevents your cookies from losing their shape. If you want to make cookies that look like the ones pictured here, see *Sally Says* below.

PREP TIME: 1 hour   **TOTAL TIME:** 4 hours   **YIELD:** 28 (3-inch, or 7.5 cm) cookies

2¼ cups (270 g) all-purpose flour, plus more if needed for dough and for rolling out

½ teaspoon baking powder

¼ teaspoon salt

¾ cup (1½ sticks, or 180 g) unsalted butter, softened to room temperature

¾ cup (150 g) granulated sugar

1 large egg, room temperature

2 teaspoons pure vanilla extract

Traditional Royal Icing (page 15) or Glaze Icing (page 14)

Sally Says

Want to make cookies that look like donuts, too? I used a 3-inch (7.5 cm) round cookie cutter for the overall cookie and a 1-inch (2.5 cm) round cookie cutter for the holes. I used Traditional Royal Icing (page 15) on the pictured cookies and a Wilton® #5 Round Decorating Tip for decorating.

1. Whisk the flour, baking powder, and salt together in a medium bowl. Set aside.

2. In a large bowl, using a handheld mixer or a stand mixer fitted with a paddle attachment, beat the butter on medium-high speed until smooth, about 1 minute. Add the granulated sugar and beat on medium-high speed until creamed, about 2 minutes. Add the egg and vanilla extract, and beat on high speed until combined, about 1 minute. Scrape down the sides and up the bottom of the bowl and beat again as needed to combine.

3. Add the dry ingredients to the wet ingredients and mix on low speed until combined. If the dough seems too soft, you can add 1 tablespoon (15 ml) more flour to make it a better consistency for rolling.

4. Divide the dough into 2 equal portions. Roll each portion out onto a piece of parchment paper or a lightly floured silicone baking mat (I prefer the nonstick silicone mat) to about ¼ inch (6 mm) thickness. The rolled-out dough can be any shape, as long as it is evenly ¼ inch (6 mm) thick.

5. Stack the 2 slabs of dough, with a piece of parchment paper between them, onto a baking sheet and refrigerate for at least 1 hour (and up to 2 days). If chilling for more than 2 hours, cover the top layer of dough with a single piece of parchment paper.

6. Preheat oven to 350°F (180°C). Line baking sheets with parchment paper or silicone baking mats.

7. Remove one of the slabs of dough from the refrigerator and, using a cookie cutter, cut into shapes. Place shapes 3 inches (7.5 cm) apart on the baking sheets. Reroll the remainder of that slab and continue cutting until all is used. Repeat with the second slab of dough.

8. Bake for 10 to 11 minutes, until lightly browned around the edges, rotating the baking sheets halfway through the bake time. Allow the cookies to cool on the baking sheets for 5 minutes, then transfer to a wire rack to cool completely before decorating. Decorate with desired icing. Let set for 2 to 3 hours.

9. Decorated cookies will stay fresh in an airtight container at room temperature or in the refrigerator for up to 1 week.

MAKE-AHEAD TIP

You can chill the rolled-out cookie dough in the refrigerator for up to 2 days (see step 5), but you can also freeze the cookie dough (before rolling out in step 4) for up to 3 months. If you opt for the latter, allow the dough to thaw overnight in the refrigerator, then bring to room temperature before rolling out; in this situation, when you get to step 5, chill the dough for only 30 minutes as opposed to 1 hour. Undecorated cookies freeze well for up to 3 months; before icing or serving, thaw overnight in the refrigerator. I do not recommend freezing with icing on top.

Chocolate Sugar Cookies

Where there is vanilla, there must be chocolate! This sugar cookie dough is flavored with cocoa and is very easy to work with. Before rolling out the dough on parchment paper or a silicone baking mat in step 4, dust the surface with a little cocoa powder. The cocoa helps prevent the dough from sticking and gives the cookies a little extra flavor!

PREP TIME: 1 hour   **TOTAL TIME:** 4 hours   **YIELD:** 28 (3-inch, or 7.5 cm) cookies

1½ cups (180 g) all-purpose flour, plus more for work surface and rolling out

¾ cup (65 g) unsweetened natural or Dutch-process cocoa powder, plus more for dusting

1 teaspoon baking powder

¼ teaspoon salt

¾ cup (1½ sticks, or 180 g) unsalted butter, softened to room temperature

1 cup (200 g) granulated sugar

1 large egg, room temperature

1 teaspoon pure vanilla extract

Traditional Royal Icing (page 15) or Glaze Icing (page 14)

MAKE-AHEAD TIP

See Cookie Cutter Sugar Cookies (page 33).

 ### Sally Says
To create cookies that look like ice cream cones, use a 4-inch (10 cm) ice cream cone cookie cutter. I used Traditional Royal Icing (page 15) on the pictured cookies and a Wilton® #5 Round Decorating Tip for decorating.

1. Whisk the flour, cocoa powder, baking powder, and salt together in a medium bowl. Set aside.

2. In a large bowl, using a handheld mixer or a stand mixer fitted with a paddle attachment, beat the butter on medium-high speed until smooth, about 1 minute. Add the granulated sugar and beat on medium-high speed until creamed, about 2 minutes. Add the egg and vanilla extract, and beat on high speed until combined, about 1 minute. Scrape down the sides and up the bottom of the bowl and beat again as needed to combine.

3. Add the dry ingredients to the wet ingredients and mix on low speed until combined. The cookie dough will be slightly sticky.

4. Divide the dough into 2 equal portions. Roll each portion out onto a piece of parchment paper or a lightly floured silicone baking mat (I prefer the nonstick silicone mat) to about ¼ inch (6 mm) thickness. The rolled-out dough can be any shape, as long as it is evenly ¼ inch (6 mm) thick.

5. Stack the 2 slabs of dough, with a piece of parchment paper between them, onto a baking sheet and refrigerate for at least 1 hour (and up to 2 days). If chilling for more than 2 hours, cover the top layer of dough with a single piece of parchment paper.

6. Once the dough is chilled, preheat oven to 350°F (180°C). Line baking sheets with parchment paper or silicone baking mats.

7. Remove one of the slabs of dough from the refrigerator and, using a cookie cutter, cut into shapes. Place shapes 3 inches (7.5 cm) apart on the baking sheets. Reroll the remainder of that slab and continue cutting until all is used. Repeat with the second slab of dough.

8. Bake for 10 to 11 minutes, until lightly browned around the edges, rotating the baking sheets halfway through the bake time. Allow the cookies to cool on the baking sheets for 5 minutes, then transfer to a wire rack to cool completely before decorating.

9. Decorate with desired icing. Let set for 2 to 3 hours.

10. Decorated cookies will stay fresh, covered, at room temperature or in the refrigerator for up to 1 week.

Jude & Franklin's Favorite Dog Biscuits

Because the pups are part of the family, too! The ingredients in this recipe have been approved by our veterinarian. Before preparing, please check with your veterinarian about any concerns or questions you have or about any possible allergies your dog may have.

PREP TIME: 20 minutes   **TOTAL TIME:** 1 hour 10 minutes   **YIELD:** 26 to 30 (3-inch, or 7.5 cm) dog biscuits

½ cup (113 g) canned pumpkin purée (not pumpkin pie filling)

½ cup (130 g) creamy peanut butter

1 large egg

2 cups (240 g) whole-wheat flour, plus more for work surface and rolling out

1 to 2 tablespoons (15 to 30 ml) milk, as needed

MAKE-AHEAD TIP

Baked biscuits freeze well up to 3 months; thaw overnight in the refrigerator before feeding to your pup.

1. Preheat oven to 350°F (180°C). Line baking sheets with parchment paper or silicone baking mats. Set aside.

2. Whisk the pumpkin purée, peanut butter, and egg together until combined. Stir in the flour. If the dough isn't coming together, add 1 to 2 tablespoons (15 to 30 ml) of milk. The dough will be very thick and a little sandy.

3. On a lightly floured surface, roll the dough out to about ¼ inch (6 mm) thickness. The rolled-out dough can be any shape, as long as it is evenly ¼ inch (6 mm) thick. Using a cookie cutter, cut into shapes. Reroll the remaining dough and continue cutting until all is used.

4. Place biscuits 3 inches (7.5 cm) apart on the baking sheets.

5. Bake for 16 to 18 minutes, or until lightly browned on the sides.

6. Remove from the oven and allow the biscuits to cool on the baking sheets for 5 minutes before transferring to a wire rack to cool completely.

7. Biscuits will stay fresh, covered, at room temperature for 1 week or in the refrigerator for up to 2 weeks.

ALL ABOUT OATS

This chapter focuses on one of the most common ingredients in cookies: oats! After chocolate chip cookies, oatmeal cookies finish second in the category of most loved cookie. While a bowl of plain oatmeal can be boring, I assure you the recipes on the following pages will have you hoarding canisters of oats like nobody's business. It's time to think beyond the bowl!

But what is it about oats that makes a cookie so utterly delicious? Texture, for starters. Oats give cookies a distinctive and unique chewy factor. They also soak in moisture from cookie dough, creating delicious nooks and crannies of softness throughout. And oats lend a naturally nutty and toasty flavor to cookies, which makes it impossible to stop at eating only one.

There are many different types of oats on grocery store shelves, so make sure you grab old-fashioned whole rolled oats for the recipes in this cookbook. Don't use the quick or instant variety.

Big Chewy Oatmeal Chocolate Chip Cookies

This is my basic oatmeal cookie recipe. It's been carefully crafted to combine the perfect chew with a thick and soft center. Here we'll fill oatmeal cookies with lots of chocolate chips, both regular size and mini, so there are plenty of pockets of chocolate inside. Molasses adds a little something special, but you can leave it out if you don't have any on hand. These cookies are unapologetically large and a home run every time.

PREP TIME: 15 minutes　　**TOTAL TIME:** 1 hour 30 minutes　　**YIELD:** about 22 cookies

1½ cups (180 g) all-purpose flour

1 teaspoon baking soda

1 teaspoon salt

1 cup (2 sticks, or 240 g) unsalted butter, softened to room temperature

1 cup (225 g) packed brown sugar

½ cup (100 g) granulated sugar

2 large eggs, room temperature

1 tablespoon (20 g) unsulphured or dark molasses (optional)

2 teaspoons pure vanilla extract

3 cups (270 g) old-fashioned whole rolled oats

1¼ cups (225 g) semi-sweet chocolate chips, plus more for topping

½ cup (90 g) mini semi-sweet chocolate chips, plus more for topping

MAKE-AHEAD TIP

See page 12.

1. Whisk the flour, baking soda, and salt together in a medium bowl. Set aside.

2. In a large bowl, using a handheld mixer or a stand mixer fitted with a paddle attachment, beat the butter on medium-high speed until smooth, about 1 minute. Add the brown sugar and granulated sugar, and beat on medium-high speed until creamed, about 2 minutes. Add the eggs, molasses (if using), and vanilla extract, and beat on high speed until combined, about 1 minute. Scrape down the sides and up the bottom of the bowl and beat again as needed to combine.

3. Add the dry ingredients to the wet ingredients and mix on low speed until combined. With the mixer running on low speed, beat in the oats and both types of chocolate chips. The dough will be thick and sticky. Cover and chill the dough in the refrigerator for at least 45 minutes (and up to 4 days). If chilling for longer than 3 hours, allow it to sit at room temperature for at least 30 minutes before rolling and baking because the dough will be quite hard.

4. Preheat oven to 350°F (180°C). Line baking sheets with parchment paper or silicone baking mats. Set aside.

5. Scoop balls of dough, about ¼ cup (No. 16 scoop) of dough per cookie, and place 4 inches (10 cm) apart on the baking sheets. Bake for 14 to 15 minutes, or until lightly browned on the sides. The centers will look very soft.

6. Remove from the oven and allow the cookies to cool on the baking sheets for 5 minutes before transferring to a wire rack to cool completely. While the cookies are still warm, I like to press a few more chocolate chips into the tops—this is only for looks!

7. Cookies will stay fresh in an airtight container at room temperature for up to 1 week.

Autumn Spice Oatmeal Cookies

This recipe is similar to my Big Chewy Oatmeal Chocolate Chip Cookies (page 41), but has some added flavors and a little less sugar because the coconut adds sweetness. These cookies may be full of autumn favorites, such as pumpkin pie spice, cinnamon, dried cranberries, and more, but they will hit the spot any time of year!

PREP TIME: 15 minutes   **TOTAL TIME:** 1 hour 30 minutes   **YIELD:** 30 cookies

1½ cups (180 g) all-purpose flour

1 teaspoon baking soda

1½ teaspoons pumpkin pie spice

1 teaspoon ground cinnamon

1 teaspoon salt

1 cup (2 sticks, or 240 g) unsalted butter, softened to room temperature

1 cup (225 g) packed brown sugar

¼ cup (50 g) granulated sugar

2 large eggs, room temperature

1 tablespoon (20 g) unsulphured or dark molasses (optional)

2 teaspoons pure vanilla extract

3 cups (270 g) old-fashioned whole rolled oats

1 cup (180 g) dark chocolate chips

¾ cup (70 g) shredded sweetened coconut

¾ cup (115 g) dried cranberries

½ cup (115 g) pepitas (shelled pumpkin seeds)

 ## Sally Says

You can play around with the add-ins. Maybe pumpkin seeds aren't your thing? Leave them out and add some chopped walnuts instead.

1. Whisk the flour, baking soda, pumpkin pie spice, cinnamon, and salt together in a medium bowl. Set aside.

2. In a large bowl, using a handheld mixer or a stand mixer fitted with a paddle attachment, beat the butter on medium-high speed until smooth, about 1 minute. Add the brown sugar and granulated sugar, and beat on medium-high speed until creamed, about 2 minutes. Add the eggs, molasses (if using), and vanilla extract, and beat on high speed until combined, about 1 minute. Scrape down the sides and up the bottom of the bowl and beat again as needed to combine.

3. Add the dry ingredients to the wet ingredients and mix on low speed until combined. With the mixer running on low speed, beat in the oats. Once combined, fold in the chocolate chips, coconut, cranberries, and pepitas. The dough will be thick and sticky. Cover and chill the dough in the refrigerator for at least 45 minutes (and up to 4 days). If chilling for longer than 3 hours, allow it to sit at room temperature for at least 30 minutes before rolling and baking because the dough will be quite hard.

4. Preheat oven to 350°F (180°C). Line baking sheets with parchment paper or silicone baking mats. Set aside.

5. Scoop balls of dough, about 2 tablespoons (No. 30 scoop) of dough per cookie, and place 2 inches (5 cm) apart on the baking sheets. Bake for 13 to 14 minutes, or until lightly browned on the sides. The centers will look a little soft.

6. Remove from the oven and allow the cookies to cool on the baking sheets for 5 minutes before transferring to a wire rack to cool completely. While the cookies are still warm, I like to press a few more chocolate chips into the tops—this is only for looks!

7. Cookies will stay fresh in an airtight container at room temperature for up to 1 week.

MAKE-AHEAD TIP

See page 12.

KITCHEN SINK COOKIES

Have you ever heard of kitchen sink cookies? They're basically a cookie with everything but the kitchen sink stuffed inside. We're talking crushed potato chips, M&M's®, oats, butterscotch morsels, nuts, and more. They're oh-so chewy with lots of delicious chunks and absolutely no apologies. Perfect for when you want to hit all your cravings at once! This recipe is a lot like my Big Chewy Oatmeal Chocolate Chip Cookies (page 41), but I use a little more sugar and add-ins.

PREP TIME: 15 minutes　　**TOTAL TIME:** 1 hour 30 minutes　　**YIELD:** about 45 cookies

1½ cups (180 g) all-purpose flour
1 teaspoon baking soda
1 teaspoon baking powder
1 teaspoon salt
1 cup (2 sticks, 240 g) unsalted butter, softened to room temperature
1½ cups (340 g) packed brown sugar
¾ cup (150 g) granulated sugar
2 large eggs, room temperature
1 tablespoon (15 ml) milk
2 teaspoons pure vanilla extract
3 cups (270 g) old-fashioned whole rolled oats
1 cup (55 g) crushed potato chips
¾ cup (180 g) butterscotch morsels, plus more for topping
¾ cup (135 g) semi-sweet chocolate chips, plus more for topping
¾ cup (126 g) mini M&M's®
¾ cup (90 g) chopped walnuts

MAKE-AHEAD TIP

See page 12.

SALLY SAYS

To keep the cookies thick but light, I added baking powder and a little extra baking soda.

1. Whisk the flour, baking soda, baking powder, and salt together in a medium bowl. Set aside.

2. In a large bowl, using a handheld mixer or a stand mixer fitted with a paddle attachment, beat the butter on medium-high speed until smooth, about 1 minute. Add the brown sugar and granulated sugar, and beat on medium-high speed until creamed, about 2 minutes. Add the eggs, milk, and vanilla extract, and beat on high speed until combined, about 1 minute. Scrape down the sides and up the bottom of the bowl and beat again as needed to combine.

3. Add the dry ingredients to the wet ingredients and mix on low speed until combined. With the mixer running on low speed, beat in the oats. Once combined, beat in the potato chips, butterscotch morsels, chocolate chips, M&M's®, and walnuts. The dough will be thick and sticky. Cover and chill the dough in the refrigerator for at least 45 minutes (and up to 4 days). If chilling for longer than 3 hours, allow it to sit at room temperature for at least 30 minutes before rolling and baking because the dough will be quite hard.

4. Preheat oven to 350°F (180°C). Line baking sheets with parchment paper or silicone baking mats. Set aside.

5. Scoop balls of dough, about 1½ tablespoons (No. 40 scoop) of dough per cookie, and place 3 inches (7.5 cm) apart on the baking sheets. Bake for 12 to 13 minutes, or until lightly browned on the sides. The centers will look very soft.

6. Remove from the oven and allow the cookies to cool on the baking sheets for 5 minutes before transferring to a wire rack to cool completely. While the cookies are still warm, I like to press a few more chocolate chips and/or butterscotch morsels into the tops—this is only for looks!

7. Cookies will stay fresh in an airtight container at room temperature for up to 1 week.

Favorite Oatmeal Raisin Cookies

If you read my blog, you're likely aware of my affinity for raisins. I love them in carrot cake, spice cake, bread, bagels, and more. This is not a joke; raisins are the BEST addition to baked goods. I know some of you out there agree . . . yes? Even if you're not a fan, I'm certain this recipe will sway your opinion. A bold promise for a simple cookie. Try it!

PREP TIME: 15 minutes   **TOTAL TIME:** 1 hour 45 minutes   **YIELD:** 30 cookies

1½ cups (180 g) all-purpose flour
1 teaspoon baking soda
1½ teaspoons ground cinnamon
1 teaspoon salt
1 cup (2 sticks, or 240 g) unsalted butter, softened to room temperature
1 cup (225 g) packed brown sugar
½ cup (100 g) granulated sugar
2 large eggs, room temperature
1 tablespoon (20 g) unsulphured or dark molasses (optional)
2 teaspoons pure vanilla extract
3 cups (270 g) old-fashioned whole rolled oats
1½ cups (220 g) raisins
½ cup (60 g) chopped walnuts

MAKE-AHEAD TIP

See page 12.

1. Whisk the flour, baking soda, cinnamon, and salt together in a medium bowl. Set aside.

2. In a large bowl, using a handheld mixer or a stand mixer fitted with a paddle attachment, beat the butter on medium-high speed until smooth, about 1 minute. Add the brown sugar and granulated sugar, and beat on medium-high speed until creamed, about 2 minutes. Add the eggs, molasses (if using), and vanilla extract, and beat on high speed until combined, about 1 minute. Scrape down the sides and up the bottom of the bowl and beat again as needed to combine.

3. Add the dry ingredients to the wet ingredients and mix on low speed until combined. With the mixer running on low speed, beat in the oats, raisins, and walnuts. The dough will be thick and sticky. Cover and chill the dough in the refrigerator for at least 1 hour (and up to 4 days). If chilling for longer than 3 hours, allow it to sit at room temperature for at least 30 minutes before rolling and baking because the dough will be quite hard.

4. Preheat oven to 350°F (180°C). Line baking sheets with parchment paper or silicone baking mats. Set aside.

5. Scoop balls of dough, about 2 tablespoons (No. 30 scoop) of dough per cookie, and place 2 inches (5 cm) apart on the baking sheets. Bake for 12 to 13 minutes, or until lightly browned on the sides. The centers will look a little soft.

6. Remove from the oven and allow to cool on baking sheets for 5 minutes before transferring to a wire rack to cool completely.

7. Cookies will stay fresh in an airtight container at room temperature for up to 1 week.

Monster Cookies

For all the times we have monstrous peanut butter . . . and chocolate . . . and oatmeal cookie cravings.
Cough *every day* cough.

PREP TIME: 20 minutes   **TOTAL TIME:** 1 hour 10 minutes   **YIELD:** 32 cookies

1½ cups (180 g) all-purpose flour

1 teaspoon baking powder

1 teaspoon baking soda

1 teaspoon salt

1 cup (2 sticks, or 240 g) unsalted
   butter, softened to room temperature

1 cup (200 g) granulated sugar

½ cup (115 g) packed brown sugar

2 large eggs, room temperature

1 cup (260 g) creamy peanut butter

2 teaspoons pure vanilla extract

2 cups (180 g) old-fashioned whole
   rolled oats

1½ cups (252 g) mini or regular-size
   M&M's®, plus more for topping

1 cup (180 g) semi-sweet chocolate
   chips, plus more for topping

MAKE-AHEAD TIP

See page 12.

1. Whisk the flour, baking powder, baking soda, and salt together in a medium bowl. Set aside.

2. In a large bowl, using a handheld mixer or a stand mixer fitted with a paddle attachment, beat the butter on medium-high speed until smooth, about 1 minute. Add the granulated sugar and brown sugar, and beat on medium-high speed until creamed, about 2 minutes. Add the eggs, peanut butter, and vanilla extract, and beat on high speed until combined, about 1 minute. Scrape down the sides and up the bottom of the bowl and beat again as needed to combine.

3. Add the dry ingredients to the wet ingredients and mix on low speed until combined. With the mixer running on low speed, add the oats. Once combined, beat in the M&M's® and chocolate chips. The dough will be thick and sticky. Cover and chill the dough in the refrigerator for at least 20 minutes (and up to 4 days). If chilling for longer than 1 hour, allow it to sit at room temperature for at least 30 minutes before rolling and baking because the dough will be quite hard.

4. Preheat oven to 350°F (180°C). Line baking sheets with parchment paper or silicone baking mats. Set aside.

5. Scoop balls of dough, 2 tablespoons (No. 30 scoop) of dough per cookie, and place 3 inches (7.5 cm) apart on the baking sheets. Bake for 12 to 14 minutes, until lightly browned on the sides. The centers will look very soft.

6. Remove from the oven and allow to cool on baking sheets for 5 minutes before transferring to a wire rack to cool completely. While the cookies are still warm, I like to press a few more chocolate chips and/or M&M's® into the tops—this is only for looks!

7. Cookies will stay fresh in an airtight container at room temperature for up to 1 week.

Iced Carrot Cake Oatmeal Cookies

Carrot cake is one of my all-time favorite flavors. This cookie has everything I love about this spiced cake in oatmeal cookie form—and that includes cream cheese icing on top! The shredded carrot keeps these cookies extra soft and tender, and because there is added moisture in the cookie dough from it, I slightly increased the amount of flour. Remember to use freshly grated carrots, as the pre-shredded ones in the produce aisle are usually pretty dry in comparison.

PREP TIME: 20 minutes   **TOTAL TIME:** 1 hour 50 minutes   **YIELD:** 30 cookies

Cookie Dough

1½ cups (180 g) all-purpose flour
1 teaspoon baking soda
1½ teaspoons ground cinnamon
¼ teaspoon ground cloves
¼ teaspoon ground ginger
¼ teaspoon ground nutmeg
1 teaspoon salt
1 cup (2 sticks, or 240 g) unsalted
   butter, softened to room temperature
1 cup (225 g) packed brown sugar
½ cup (100 g) granulated sugar
2 large eggs, room temperature
1 tablespoon (20 g) unsulphured or dark
   molasses (optional)
2 teaspoons pure vanilla extract
1½ cups (165 g) freshly grated peeled
   carrots (about 3 to 4 large carrots)
3 cups (270 g) old-fashioned whole
   rolled oats
1 cup (120 g) chopped walnuts (optional)

Cream Cheese Icing

3 tablespoons (45 g) block cream
   cheese, softened to room temperature
1 tablespoon (15 g) unsalted butter,
   softened to room temperature
1 cup (120 g) confectioners' sugar
1 or 2 tablespoons (15 or 30 ml) milk

1. **To make the cookies:** Whisk the flour, baking soda, cinnamon, cloves, ginger, nutmeg, and salt together in a medium bowl. Set aside.

2. In a large bowl, using a handheld mixer or a stand mixer fitted with a paddle attachment, beat the butter on medium-high speed until smooth, about 1 minute. Add the brown sugar and granulated sugar, and beat on medium-high speed until creamed, about 2 minutes. Add the eggs, molasses (if using), and vanilla extract, and beat on high speed until combined, about 1 minute. Scrape down the sides and up the bottom of the bowl and beat again as needed to combine.

3. Add the dry ingredients to the wet ingredients and mix on low speed until combined. With the mixer running on low speed, beat in the carrots, oats, and, if using, walnuts. The dough will be thick and sticky. Cover and chill the dough in the refrigerator for at least 1 hour (and up to 4 days). If chilling for longer than 3 hours, allow it to sit at room temperature for at least 30 minutes before rolling and baking because the dough will be quite hard.

4. Preheat oven to 350°F (180°C). Line baking sheets with parchment paper or silicone baking mats. Set aside.

5. Scoop balls of dough, about 2 tablespoons (No. 30 scoop) of dough per cookie, and place 3 inches (7.5 cm) apart on the baking sheets. Bake for 13 to 14 minutes, or until lightly browned on the sides. The centers will look a little soft.

6. Remove from the oven and allow to cool on baking sheets for 5 minutes before transferring to a wire rack to cool completely.

7. **To make the icing:** In a medium bowl, using a handheld mixer or a stand mixer fitted with a whisk attachment, beat the cream cheese and butter together on medium-high speed until completely smooth. Add the confectioners' sugar and 1 tablespoon (15 ml) of the milk, and beat on low speed until it all comes together. Beat in an extra tablespoon (15 ml) of milk to thin it out, if needed.

Sally Says

I love LOTS of spice flavor in carrot cake. If you crave extra spice flavor like I do, increase amounts to 2 teaspoons ground cinnamon and ½ teaspoon each of the ground cloves, ground ginger, and ground nutmeg.

8. Dip the top of each completely cooled cookie into icing.

9. Iced cookies will stay fresh in an airtight container at room temperature for 2 days or in the refrigerator for up to 1 week.

MAKE-AHEAD TIP

See page 12 for making the dough ahead of time. Unfrosted baked cookies can be frozen for up to 3 months; allow to thaw in the refrigerator overnight, then continue with step 7.

Banana Almond Berry Breakfast Cookies

There is a time and place for cookies and, sadly, this does not typically include breakfast. However, when only wholesome ingredients are involved, I say eating cookies for breakfast is not only a genius way to jump-start the day, but a tasty one, too! They are soft, hearty, and not overly sweet, and only use one bowl. Use certified gluten-free oats, for gluten-free cookies.

PREP TIME: 10 minutes   **TOTAL TIME:** 50 minutes   **YIELD:** 12 cookies

2 ripe bananas
2½ cups (225 g) old-fashioned whole rolled oats
1 cup (250 g) almond butter, room temperature
⅓ cup (170 g) honey
½ cup (45 g) sliced almonds
½ cup (75 g) dried cranberries
½ teaspoon pure vanilla extract
½ teaspoon ground cinnamon
¼ teaspoon salt

MAKE-AHEAD TIP

Baked cookies freeze well for up to 3 months; thaw overnight in the refrigerator and, if desired, bring to room temperature before serving.

1. Preheat oven to 325°F (170°C). Line baking sheets with parchment paper or silicone baking mats. Set aside.

2. Mash the bananas easily using a handheld or stand mixer fitted with a paddle attachment. Once the bananas are mashed, add the almond butter, honey, sliced almonds, cranberries, vanilla extract, cinnamon, and salt. Beat together on medium speed until everything is combined.

3. Scoop mounds of the mixture, about ¼ cup (No. 16 scoop) of the mixture per cookie, and place 3 inches (7.5 cm) apart on the baking sheets. You won't want to have more than 6 cookies per baking sheet since they are so large. The cookies won't spread much in the oven, so gently press the mounds down to create a flatter shape.

4. Bake for 17 to 20 minutes, until lightly browned on the sides.

5. Remove from the oven and allow to cool on baking sheets for 5 minutes before transferring to a wire rack to cool completely.

6. Cookies will stay fresh in an airtight container at room temperature or in the refrigerator for up to 1 week.

 ## Sally Says

I like to make a batch of these breakfast cookies a couple times per month and wrap them individually so they're portioned out.

Nutella® No-Bakes

I married into a family known for their chocolate peanut butter no-bake cookies. They're my husband's favorite, and I posted the recipe on my blog a couple years ago. These cookies are outstanding—and couldn't be easier! When brainstorming recipes for this cookbook, I knew I had to include some form of this family favorite. Kevin's always hinted at a Nutella® version, so we worked on this one together. I love them with a little sea salt on top!

PREP TIME: 15 minutes   **TOTAL TIME:** 1 hour 15 minutes   **YIELD:** 36 cookies

½ cup (120 ml) milk (I use 2% or whole)
¼ cup (½ stick, or 60 g) unsalted butter
1½ cups (300 g) granulated sugar
1 cup (300 g) Nutella®
1 teaspoon pure vanilla extract
2¾ cups (245 g) old-fashioned whole rolled oats
coarse sea salt, for topping (optional)

MAKE-AHEAD TIP

You can prepare the mixture in step 1, cover tightly, and store in the refrigerator for up to 3 days. The mixture will be very firm after refrigeration, so bring to room temperature before continuing with the recipe. The no-bake cookies prepared through step 4 can be frozen for up to 3 months; thaw overnight in the refrigerator before serving.

1. Combine the milk, butter, and granulated sugar in a medium saucepan over medium heat. Whisk until the butter melts, then bring to a boil. Allow to boil for 1 minute without whisking. Remove from heat and stir in the Nutella® and vanilla extract until completely combined. Add the oats and stir together until everything is combined.

2. Line baking sheets with parchment paper or silicone baking mats. Make sure there is enough room in your refrigerator for the baking sheets.

3. Scoop balls of dough, about 1 tablespoon (No. 60 scoop) of the mixture per cookie, and place 2 inches (5 cm) apart on the lined baking sheets. If desired, slightly flatten each one out and/or lightly sprinkle with sea salt.

4. Refrigerate the cookies for at least 30 minutes before enjoying.

5. Cookies will stay fresh in an airtight container in the refrigerator for up to 1 week.

Happy Holidays

Every holiday season, the memories of previous Decembers come flooding back. The smell of fresh pine, the sounds of family visiting, and the sight of stockings on the mantel—it's the little things that make this time of year so special. But going through this season without fresh-baked cookies would be like celebrating the Fourth of July without fireworks, or your birthday without cake. Along with family, love, and tradition, cookies make up the fabric of the winter holiday season. That's why this chapter is the longest in the book. It just isn't the holidays without a batch—or eleven batches—of cookies!

The following pages are filled with kid-friendly holiday favorites and treats perfect for your cookie exchanges and festive parties. There are classic holiday cookies, such as gingerbread and chocolate crinkles, as well as my family's traditional favorites, including snowballs, pecan tassies, and coconut macaroons. Another holiday favorite you have to try is my recipe for Cookie Cutter Sugar Cookies on page 32. Don't forget to pick up some snowflake and Christmas tree–shaped cookie cutters before you get started!

The happiest (and tastiest!) of holidays start here.

GINGERBREAD COOKIES

No matter how you shape them, gingerbread cookies are a necessity each holiday season. This recipe has been my staple for the past several years. The cookies not only hold their shape, but feature impeccable spice and molasses flavors, crisp edges, and soft centers.

PREP TIME: 1 hour   **TOTAL TIME:** 4 hours 30 minutes   **YIELD:** 24 (4-inch, or 10 cm) cookies

3½ cups (420 g) all-purpose flour, plus more for work surface and rolling out

1 teaspoon baking soda

½ teaspoon salt

1 tablespoon (15 ml) ground ginger (yes, 1 full tablespoon!)

1 tablespoon (15 ml) ground cinnamon

½ teaspoon allspice

½ teaspoon ground cloves

10 tablespoons (1¼ sticks, or 150 g) unsalted butter, softened to room temperature

¾ cup (170 g) packed brown sugar

1 large egg, room temperature

⅔ cup (225 g) unsulphured or dark molasses

1 teaspoon pure vanilla extract

Traditional Royal Icing (page 15) or Glaze Icing (page 14)

MAKE-AHEAD TIP

You can chill the cookie dough discs in the refrigerator for up to 4 days or you can freeze them for up to 3 months; if you opt for the latter, allow the discs to thaw overnight in the refrigerator, then bring to room temperature before rolling out. Undecorated baked cookies freeze well for up to 3 months; before serving, thaw overnight in the refrigerator, then decorate them, if desired. I do not recommend freezing with icing on top.

1. Whisk the flour, baking soda, salt, ginger, cinnamon, allspice, and cloves together in a medium bowl. Set aside.

2. In a large bowl, using a handheld mixer or a stand mixer fitted with a paddle attachment, beat the butter on medium-high speed until smooth, about 1 minute. Add the brown sugar and beat on medium-high speed until creamed, about 2 minutes. Add the egg, molasses, and vanilla extract, and beat on high speed until combined, about 1 minute. Scrape down the sides and up the bottom of the bowl and beat again as needed to combine.

3. Add the dry ingredients to the wet ingredients and mix on low speed until combined. The cookie dough will be quite thick and slightly sticky.

4. Divide the dough into 2 equal portions, then place each portion onto a large piece of plastic wrap. Wrap each one tightly and pat down to create a disc shape. Chill discs in the refrigerator for at least 3 hours (and up to 4 days).

5. Preheat oven to 350°F (180°C). Line baking sheets with parchment paper or silicone baking mats. Set aside.

6. Remove 1 disc of chilled cookie dough from the refrigerator. Generously flour a work surface, as well as your hands and the rolling pin. The dough may still be sticky, so keep extra flour nearby to use as needed. Roll out the disc until it's ¼ inch (6 mm) thick. Cut into shapes using cookie cutters. Place shapes 3 inches (7.5 cm) apart on prepared baking sheets. Reroll dough scraps and continue cutting into shapes until all of the dough has been used. Repeat with the remaining disc of dough.

7. Bake cookies for about 10 to 11 minutes, until they show small cracks on top. If your cookie cutters are smaller than 4 inches (10 cm), bake for about 9 minutes.

8. Remove from the oven and allow to cool on baking sheets for 5 minutes before transferring to a wire rack to cool completely.

9. Once cookies are completely cooled, decorate with desired icing. Let set for 2 to 3 hours.

10. Whether decorated or left plain, cookies will stay fresh, covered, at room temperature or in the refrigerator for up to 1 week.

Chocolate Peppermint Biscotti

It doesn't need to be the holidays to enjoy these holly jolly biscotti! Making biscotti may seem daunting, but the process is anything but. These cookies are twice-baked, which contributes to their traditional crunchy coffee-soaker-upper texture. That's a term, correct? Crushed candy canes add to the festive fun!

PREP TIME: 40 minutes   **TOTAL TIME:** 2 hours   **YIELD:** 32 cookies

1¾ cups (210 g) all-purpose flour, plus more for work surface and hands

½ cup (43 g) unsweetened natural cocoa powder

1 cup (200 g) granulated sugar

1 teaspoon baking soda

½ teaspoon salt

5 tablespoons (75 g) butter, cold and cubed

4 large eggs, room temperature, divided

1 teaspoon pure vanilla extract

1 teaspoon peppermint extract

1 cup (270 g) mini or regular-size semi-sweet chocolate chips

1 tablespoon (15 ml) milk

4-ounce (113 g) bar semi-sweet chocolate, coarsely chopped

½ cup crushed candy canes

1. Preheat oven to 350°F (180°C). Line baking sheets with parchment paper or silicone baking mats. Set aside.

2. Whisk the flour, cocoa powder, granulated sugar, baking soda, and salt together in a large bowl. Using a pastry cutter or your hands, cut in the butter until the mixture is crumbly. Set aside.

3. In a small bowl, whisk 3 of the eggs, vanilla extract, and peppermint extract together. Pour into the flour-butter mixture, then gently mix with a large spoon or rubber spatula until everything is just barely moistened. Fold in the chocolate chips.

4. Turn the dough out onto a lightly floured surface and, with floured hands, knead lightly until the dough is soft and slightly sticky, about 8 to 10 times. If it's very sticky, knead 1 to 2 more tablespoon(s), or 8 to 15 g, of flour into the dough. With floured hands, divide the dough into 2 equal portions and place each portion onto its own cookie sheet. Shape each portion into an 8-inch-long (20 cm) slab, patting down until each is about ½ inch (13 mm) thick.

5. In a small bowl, beat the remaining egg with the milk. Using a pastry brush, lightly brush the top and sides of each slab of dough with the egg wash.

6. Bake the slabs of dough for 20 minutes. Remove from the oven, but do not turn off the heat. Allow slabs to cool for 10 minutes. Once the slabs are cool enough to handle, cut each into 1-inch-thick (2.5 cm) slices (see photo, left). Set slices, cut sides facing up, ¼ inch (6 mm) apart on the baking sheets.

7. Return to the oven to continue baking for 8 to 9 minutes. Turn the biscotti over and bake for another 5 to 6 minutes. The biscotti will be slightly soft in the center with harder edges. Remove from the oven and allow to cool for 5 minutes on the cookie sheets.

8. Transfer biscotti to a wire rack to cool completely. As they cool, the biscotti will become crunchy.

MAKE-AHEAD TIP

Biscotti can be frozen for up to
3 months, but I suggest freezing
without the chocolate drizzle; allow
to thaw in the refrigerator overnight,
then drizzle with chocolate 30 minutes
prior to serving.

9. Melt the chopped chocolate in a double boiler or in the microwave
    in 15-second increments, stopping and stirring after each until
    completely smooth. Drizzle biscotti with chocolate and sprinkle with
    crushed candy canes.

10. Allow the chocolate to set in the refrigerator or at room temperature,
    about 30 minutes, before enjoying. Cookies will stay fresh in an
    airtight container at room temperature for up to 10 days.

Pinwheel Cookies

Hypnotizing, right? These classic butter cookies are a Christmas cookie–tray staple! They're made by layering and rolling chocolate and vanilla dough together. What I love most about this particular pinwheel recipe—straight from my family's kitchen—is that both flavors are made from the same cookie dough. We'll add some melted chocolate and an extra dose of flour to prepare the chocolate version. I used to have trouble with the cookies spreading too much in the oven, but once I began chilling the dough in step 5 and again in step 8, the cookies started holding their shape beautifully. Learn from my mistake!

PREP TIME: 30 minutes   **TOTAL TIME:** 5 hours   **YIELD:** 24 cookies

2½ cups (300 g) plus 1 tablespoon (15 ml) all-purpose flour
½ teaspoon baking powder
½ teaspoon salt
1 cup (2 sticks, or 240 g) unsalted butter, softened to room temperature
1 cup (200 g) granulated sugar
2 large eggs, room temperature, divided (see *Sally Says*, below)
2 teaspoons pure vanilla extract
2 ounces (56 g) semi-sweet chocolate, melted and slightly cooled
1 tablespoon (15 ml) water

Sally Says

This recipe calls for 2 eggs. You'll need 1 whole egg plus 1 egg yolk for the cookie dough in step 2, and 1 egg white to brush onto the vanilla dough in step 7.

1. Whisk 2½ cups (300 g) of the flour, the baking powder, and the salt together in a medium bowl. Set aside.

2. In a large bowl, using a handheld mixer or a stand mixer fitted with a paddle attachment, beat the butter on medium-high speed until smooth, about 1 minute. Add the granulated sugar and beat on medium-high speed until creamed, about 2 minutes. Add 1 whole egg, 1 egg yolk (reserve remaining egg white), and vanilla extract, and beat on high speed until combined, about 1 minute. Scrape down the sides and up the bottom of the bowl and beat again as needed to combine.

3. Add the dry ingredients to the wet ingredients and mix on low speed until combined.

4. Divide the dough into 2 equal portions. It's helpful to use a kitchen scale for accuracy. Place one portion aside. Place the other portion back into the mixing bowl. Beat in the remaining 1 tablespoon (15 ml) flour on medium speed until combined, then add the chocolate. Beat on medium-high speed until completely combined.

5. Shape each portion of the dough into a 4 × 4-inch (10 × 10 cm) square and wrap each tightly in plastic wrap. Chill in the refrigerator for at least 2 hours (and up to 4 days).

6. Whisk the reserved egg white and the water together. Set aside.

7. Remove the vanilla dough from the refrigerator and roll out into a 9 × 12-inch (23 × 30 cm) rectangle on a piece of parchment paper. Remove the chocolate dough from the refrigerator and roll out into a rectangle slightly smaller than the first—about 8½ × 11½ inches (22 × 29 cm). Brush egg white glaze lightly on the vanilla dough. This helps the two flavors of dough stick together. Place the chocolate dough on top of the vanilla dough, using the parchment paper to help transport.

continued »

8. Starting with a long edge, use the parchment paper under the vanilla dough to help roll the 2 doughs together. Make sure the doughs are rolled tightly together, with no gaps between them. Cut the log in half so you have two 6-inch (15 cm) logs. Wrap each log tightly in plastic wrap and chill in the refrigerator for at least 2 more hours.

9. Preheat oven to 350°F (180°C). Line baking sheets with parchment paper or silicone baking mats. Set aside.

10. Remove the logs from the refrigerator, unwrap each, and slice into ½-inch (13 mm) slices (see photo, left). If dough becomes too soft, place back in the refrigerator for 10 more minutes. Place the cookies 3 inches (7.5 cm) apart on baking sheets.

11. Bake until very lightly browned on the edges, 12 to 14 minutes.

12. Remove from the oven and allow to cool on baking sheets for 5 minutes before transferring to a wire rack to cool completely.

13. Cookies will stay fresh in an airtight container at room temperature for up to 1 week.

MAKE-AHEAD TIP

Baked pinwheel cookies freeze well for up to 3 months; allow cookies to thaw overnight in the refrigerator, then bring to room temperature before serving. Raw cookie dough logs also freeze well for up to 3 months; allow the logs to thaw overnight in the refrigerator, then continue with step 9.

Raspberry Almond Linzer Cookies

No matter what time of year it is or how you shape them, linzer cookies are completely divine because of their unique taste. The cookies in this recipe unite the flavors of almond and raspberry jam, but you can use any jam flavor you desire. The trick to the almonds? Grind them up with brown sugar, which will help prevent them from turning into straight-up almond butter and will lend added flavor to the cookies. Add a touch of cinnamon, and be sure to prepare the cookies a day ahead of time so the jam softens the cookie sandwiches.

PREP TIME: 1 hour   **TOTAL TIME:** 4 hours 30 minutes   **YIELD:** 32 cookie sandwiches

⅔ cup (95 g) whole unsalted almonds

⅔ cup (150 g) packed brown sugar, divided

2½ cups (300 g) all-purpose flour, plus more for work surface and rolling out

½ teaspoon baking powder

½ teaspoon ground cinnamon

½ teaspoon salt

1 cup (2 sticks, or 240 g) unsalted butter, softened to room temperature

1 large egg, room temperature

1½ teaspoons pure vanilla extract

½ cup (160 g) raspberry jam or jelly

2 tablespoons (30 ml) confectioners' sugar, for dusting

1. Place the almonds and ⅓ cup (75 g) of the brown sugar in the bowl of a food processor. Pulse until very fine crumbs form. Set aside.

2. Whisk the flour, baking powder, cinnamon, and salt together in a medium bowl. Set aside.

3. In a large bowl, using a handheld mixer or a stand mixer fitted with a paddle attachment, beat the butter on medium-high speed until smooth, about 1 minute. Add the remaining ⅓ cup (75 g) brown sugar and beat on medium-high speed until creamed, about 2 minutes. Add the egg and vanilla extract, and beat on high speed until combined, about 1 minute. Scrape down the sides and up the bottom of the bowl and beat again as needed to combine.

4. Add the flour mixture and the ground almond mixture to the wet ingredients and mix on low speed until combined.

5. Divide the dough into 2 equal portions and place each portion onto a large piece of plastic wrap. Wrap each one up tightly and pat down to create a disc shape. Chill the discs in the refrigerator for at least 3 hours (and up to 4 days). If chilling for longer than 3 hours, allow the dough to sit at room temperature for at least 30 minutes before rolling because the dough will be quite hard.

6. Preheat oven to 350°F (180°C). Line baking sheets with parchment paper or silicone baking mats. Set aside.

7. Remove 1 disc of chilled cookie dough from the refrigerator. Generously flour a work surface, as well as your hands and the rolling pin. The dough may become sticky as you work, so keep extra flour nearby to use as needed. Roll out the disc until ¼ inch (6 mm) thick. Using a 2-inch (5 cm) round cookie cutter, cut the dough into circles. Reroll the remaining dough and continue cutting until all is used. Repeat with the second disc of dough. You should have about 64 circles.

continued »

MAKE-AHEAD TIP

As mentioned in the recipe instructions, you can chill the cookie dough in the refrigerator for up to 4 days (see step 5), but you can also freeze it for up to 3 months. If you opt for the latter, allow the dough to thaw overnight in the refrigerator, then bring to room temperature before rolling out in step 7. Cookies freeze well for up to 3 months; thaw overnight in the refrigerator and bring to room temperature before serving.

8. Using a 1-inch (2.5 cm) round cookie cutter, cut a hole into the center of 32 of the circles. Let's call these 32 cookies the "donut cookies" because of that center hole.

9. Arrange the whole circles and the donut cookies on separate baking sheets (because the donut cookies take 1 minute less to bake), placing all cookies 2 inches (5 cm) apart from one another.

10. Bake the whole circles for about 11 minutes, or until lightly browned around the edges, and bake the donut cookies for about 10 minutes. Make sure you rotate the baking sheets halfway through the bake time. Allow the cookies to cool on the baking sheets for 5 minutes, then transfer to a wire rack to cool completely before assembling.

11. Spread ½ teaspoon of jam on each whole cookie. Carefully top each with a donut cookie and press down gently to create a cookie sandwich. Dust each with confectioners' sugar.

12. Cookies will stay fresh, covered, at room temperature for 2 days or in the refrigerator for up to 1 week.

Butter Spritz Cookies

Bite-size and oh-so festive, these buttery spritz cookies are a must for your holiday season. Have fun making different shapes with your cookie press!

PREP TIME: 30 minutes   **TOTAL TIME:** 1 hour   **YIELD:** 84 bite-size cookies

1 cup (2 sticks, or 240 g) unsalted
   butter, softened to room temperature
¾ cup (150 g) granulated sugar
1 large egg, room temperature
1 teaspoon pure vanilla extract
1 teaspoon almond extract
2¼ cups (270 g) all-purpose flour
½ teaspoon salt
sanding sugar, for decoration (optional)

Sally Says

No cookie press? No problem! Instead, use a pastry bag fitted with a ½-inch (13 mm) open star tip.

1. Preheat oven to 350°F (180°C). Line baking sheets with parchment paper or silicone baking mats. Set aside.

2. In a large bowl, using a handheld mixer or a stand mixer fitted with a paddle attachment, beat the butter on medium-high speed until smooth, about 1 minute. Add the granulated sugar and beat on medium-high speed until creamed, about 2 minutes. Add the egg, vanilla extract, and almond extract, and beat on high speed until combined, about 1 minute. Scrape down the sides and up the bottom of the bowl and beat again as needed to combine.

3. On low speed, beat in the flour and salt. Turn up to high speed and beat until completely combined.

4. Press the dough; follow manufacturer's directions to fit your cookie press with a decorative plate. Scrape some of the dough into your cookie press. Hold the cookie press perpendicular to the lined baking sheet and press out the cookies 2 inches (5 cm) apart. If desired, decorate the shaped cookie dough with sprinkles.

5. If the cookie dough becomes too soft as you work, chill the shaped cookie dough in the refrigerator for 10 minutes before baking. Bake until very lightly browned on the edges, 7 to 9 minutes.

6. Remove from the oven and allow to cool on baking sheet for 5 minutes before transferring to a wire rack to cool completely.

7. Cookies will stay fresh in an airtight container at room temperature for up to 1 week.

MAKE-AHEAD TIP

You can chill the raw cookie dough in the refrigerator for up to 4 days, and then bring to room temperature, before pressing the dough through the cookie press. You can also freeze the cookie dough for up to 3 months; allow to thaw overnight in the refrigerator, then bring to room temperature before continuing with step 4. Baked cookies freeze well for up to 3 months; thaw overnight in the refrigerator before serving.

Cherry Almond Coconut Macaroons

I have to admit something: If I had to choose a favorite cookie, it would definitely be coconut macaroons. These infinitely chewy cookies take me back to childhood. Here I jazz them up with festive cherries and a drizzle of white chocolate. A food processor is necessary to really grind up that coconut (finer coconut pieces help the macaroons stay intact). And one more thing: macaroons know no seasons, so definitely flip to this page throughout the year!

PREP TIME: 15 minutes   **TOTAL TIME:** 1 hour 30 minutes   **YIELD:** 20 to 22 cookies

14-ounce (396 g) bag sweetened shredded coconut
½ cup (100 g) granulated sugar
1 teaspoon pure vanilla extract
½ teaspoon almond extract
4 large egg whites
10 to 11 red and/or green maraschino cherries, halved
4-ounce (113 g) bar white chocolate, coarsely chopped

Sally Says

Use a cookie scoop to help divide up the dough. This dough is extremely sticky and difficult to mold into tight compact mounds without one. For a delicious chocolate macaroon, flip to page 171!

1. Preheat oven to 325°F (170°C). Line baking sheets with parchment paper or silicone baking mats. Set aside.

2. In a large food processor, pulse the coconut until very finely chopped. Add the granulated sugar, vanilla extract, and almond extract, and pulse until relatively combined. Add the egg whites and pulse until the entire mixture comes together. The mixture will be very moist and sticky.

3. Scoop balls of the mixture, about 1½ tablespoons (No. 40 scoop) per cookie, and place 2 inches (5 cm) apart on the baking sheets. Press a cherry half into the top of each ball. Bake for 18 to 21 minutes, or until lightly toasted on the edges and top.

4. Remove from the oven. Allow macaroons to cool on the baking sheets for 15 minutes before transferring to a wire rack to cool completely.

5. Melt the chopped white chocolate in a double boiler or in the microwave in 15-second increments, stopping and stirring after each until completely smooth. Drizzle over the macaroons. Allow the white chocolate to set at room temperature or in the refrigerator for about 30 minutes before enjoying.

6. Macaroons will stay fresh in an airtight container in the refrigerator for up to 1 week.

MAKE-AHEAD TIP

Prepare the macaroon mixture in step 2, then transfer to a bowl, cover tightly, and refrigerate for up to 4 days before continuing with step 3. Baked macaroons, without the white chocolate drizzle, freeze well for up to 3 months; thaw overnight in the refrigerator before drizzling the white chocolate over them and serving.

CLASSIC CHOCOLATE CRINKLES

It seems everyone has a slightly different version of this quintessential holiday cookie, and this recipe is my new favorite. For festive flavor, try mixing in ½ teaspoon of peppermint extract with the vanilla extract or 2 teaspoons of espresso powder with the dry ingredients. After one bite, these fudgy cookies will have a permanent spot in your baking repertoire!

PREP TIME: 20 minutes   **TOTAL TIME:** 50 minutes   **YIELD:** 24 to 28 cookies

1½ cups (180 g) all-purpose flour

1 cup (200 g) granulated sugar

½ cup (115 g) packed brown sugar

1½ teaspoons baking powder

½ teaspoon salt

6 tablespoons (¾ stick, or 90 g) unsalted butter, melted and slightly cooled

¾ cup (65 g) unsweetened natural or Dutch-process cocoa powder

3 large eggs, room temperature

1 teaspoon pure vanilla extract

1 cup (120 g) confectioners' sugar, for coating

1. Preheat oven to 350°F (180°C). Line baking sheets with parchment paper or silicone baking mats. Set aside.

2. Whisk the flour, granulated sugar, brown sugar, baking powder, and salt together in a large bowl. Set aside.

3. Combine the melted butter and cocoa powder in a medium bowl. The mixture will be very thick, almost like a paste. Stir in the eggs and vanilla extract. Pour into the dry ingredients and, using a handheld or stand mixer fitted with a paddle attachment, beat it all together on medium-high speed. The mixture may seem dry at first, but will come together as you continue to mix (see photo, left).

4. Measure 1 tablespoon of the dough (use a No. 60 scoop for ease if desired since the dough can be a little sticky). Gently roll into a ball, then roll each ball in confectioners' sugar to coat. Place balls 3 inches (7.5 cm) apart on the baking sheets. Bake for 12 to 13 minutes. The cookies will slightly spread and form cracks. The centers will look very soft.

5. Remove from the oven and allow to cool on baking sheets for 5 minutes before transferring to a wire rack to cool completely.

6. Cookies will stay fresh in an airtight container at room temperature for up to 1 week.

MAKE-AHEAD TIP

See page 12.

 SALLY SAYS

For this recipe, it's imperative that the eggs are at room temperature. They won't properly mix into the butter-cocoa mixture if they're cold. With regard to melting the butter, do so in the microwave or on the stovetop about 10 minutes before beginning so it has time to cool down slightly. After all, we don't want to cook the eggs!

Ginger Pistachio Cookies

Any type of ginger or molasses cookie holds a permanent spot in my top five favorite cookies. My mom's recipe, published in my first cookbook, *Sally's Baking Addiction*, has been a yearly holiday tradition probably ever since I could chew! This version, adapted from my mama's recipe, includes the addition of salty pistachios. I brought these to a Christmas party last year and everyone swarmed around them. It was like I brought a plate of gold. They're soft, salty, sweet, spiced, and total winners.

PREP TIME: 15 minutes   **TOTAL TIME:** 1 hour 50 minutes   **YIELD:** 36 cookies

2 cups (240 g) all-purpose flour

1 teaspoon baking soda

1 teaspoon ground cinnamon

1 teaspoon ground cloves

1 teaspoon ground ginger

½ teaspoon salt

¾ cup (1½ sticks, or 180 g) unsalted butter, softened to room temperature

½ cup (115 g) packed brown sugar

1 cup (200 g) granulated sugar, divided

¼ cup (80 g) unsulphured or dark molasses

1 large egg, room temperature

1 teaspoon pure vanilla extract

1 cup (125 g) finely chopped salted pistachios

MAKE-AHEAD TIP

See page 12.

1. Whisk the flour, baking soda, cinnamon, cloves, ginger, and salt together in a medium bowl. Set aside.

2. In a large bowl, using a handheld mixer or a stand mixer fitted with a paddle attachment, beat the butter on medium-high speed until smooth, about 1 minute. Add the brown sugar and ½ cup (100 g) of the granulated sugar, and beat on medium-high speed until creamed, about 2 minutes. Add the molasses, egg, and vanilla extract, and beat on high speed until combined, about 1 minute. Scrape down the sides and up the bottom of the bowl and beat again as needed to combine.

3. Add the dry ingredients to the wet ingredients and mix on low speed until combined. With the mixer running on low speed, add the pistachios. Cover and chill the dough in the refrigerator for 1 hour (and up to 4 days). If chilling for longer than 3 hours, allow it to sit at room temperature for at least 30 minutes before rolling and baking because the dough will be quite hard and the cookies may not spread.

4. Preheat oven to 350°F (180°C). Line baking sheets with parchment paper or silicone baking mats. Set aside.

5. Roll balls of dough, 1 scant tablespoon of dough per cookie, into the remaining ½ cup (100 g) granulated sugar. Place each ball 2 inches (5 cm) apart on the baking sheets. Bake for 13 minutes, or until cracked on top.

6. Remove from the oven and allow to cool on baking sheets for 5 minutes before transferring to a wire rack to cool completely.

7. Cookies will stay fresh in an airtight container at room temperature for up to 1 week.

Pecan Tassies

I'm not sure if these technically count as cookies, but they were always part of our holiday season. And you often see them at holiday cookie exchanges, so I say they're COOKIES! This recipe comes from my family. It's a tender cream cheese dough filled with brown, sugary pecan magic. The treats are baked in mini-muffin pans, and the recipe yields a lot—almost four dozen! I remember helping my mom by making the indent in the dough with my thumb before she spooned the filling inside. Remember, always keep the crust cold before baking. Make sure you have room in your refrigerator for both muffin pans before you begin.

PREP TIME: 1 hour   **TOTAL TIME:** 4 hours 30 minutes   **YIELD:** 44 to 48 cookies

Cream Cheese Dough

3 cups (360 g) all-purpose flour,
  plus more for work surface
¼ cup (50 g) granulated sugar
½ teaspoon salt
1 cup (2 sticks, or 240 g) unsalted
  butter, very cold and cubed
8 ounces (227 g) block cream cheese,
  softened to room temperature and cut
  into pieces
1 or 2 teaspoons cold water, if needed

Filling

2 large eggs, room temperature
1½ cups (340 g) packed brown sugar
2 tablespoons (30 g) unsalted butter,
  melted and slightly cooled
1 teaspoon pure vanilla extract
½ teaspoon ground cinnamon
¼ teaspoon salt
1 cup (110 g) chopped pecans

Topping

2 tablespoons (30 ml) confectioners'
  sugar, for dusting

1. **To make the dough:** Place the flour, granulated sugar, and salt in the bowl of a food processor. Pulse a couple times to blend. Add the cubed butter and cream cheese. Pulse until crumbly; this will take 30 seconds or so. Pulse until there are pea-size crumbs throughout.

2. Pour the dough onto a lightly floured work surface. Fold together with your hands. If the dough seems extremely dry, add 1 teaspoon of cold water on top and mix in. Add up to 1 more teaspoon, if needed.

3. Divide the dough into 2 equal portions, then place each portion onto a large piece of plastic wrap. Wrap each one tightly and pat down to create a disc shape. Chill in the refrigerator for at least 3 hours (and up to 1 day). If chilling for longer than 3 hours, allow the discs to sit at room temperature for at least 30 minutes before rolling and baking.

4. Lightly grease two 24-count mini-muffin pans or spray with nonstick spray.

5. Remove 1 disc of dough from the refrigerator, keeping the other in the refrigerator to stay cold. Tear off 1 tablespoon of dough, roll into a ball, and place the ball into a cup of one of the pans. Repeat with remaining dough so that all 24 cups in the first pan are filled. Press your thumb into each ball, creating a deep indent, or shell, for the filling. Place the entire pan in the refrigerator. You always want the dough cold! Repeat with the second disc of dough and mini-muffin pan.

6. Once both pans are in the refrigerator chilling, preheat oven to 375°F (190°C).

7. **To make the filling:** Whisk the eggs, brown sugar, melted butter, vanilla extract, cinnamon, and salt together in a medium bowl until combined. Fold in the chopped pecans.

continued »

8. Remove 1 muffin pan of shells from the refrigerator and fill each with filling, about ¾ to 1 teaspoon (see photo, left). Repeat with the second muffin pan of shells. Bake for 18 to 21 minutes, or until the shell edges are lightly browned and the fillings look set.

9. Remove from the oven and allow to cool for 20 minutes before removing the cookies from the pan. Once cooled, dust lightly with confectioners' sugar.

10. Cookies will stay fresh in an airtight container at room temperature for 3 days or in the refrigerator for up to 1 week.

MAKE-AHEAD TIP

You can make the dough ahead of time and store in the refrigerator for up to 1 day (as described in step 2) or freeze for up to 3 months; if you opt for the latter, thaw in the refrigerator overnight before using. You can also prepare the pecan tassies through step 7 (before baking them) and keep the shaped, unbaked pecan tassies in the refrigerator for up to 1 day before baking. Baked pecan tassies freeze well for up to 3 months; thaw overnight in the refrigerator and, if desired, bring to room temperature before serving.

SALLY SAYS

If you don't have a food processor to make the dough, you can use a whisk to mix the dry ingredients together in a large bowl and a pastry cutter to cut the cubed butter and cream cheese into the dry ingredients. Do NOT use an electric handheld or stand mixer for this dough.

CRANBERRY SPICE RUGELACH

Rugelach are more of a pastry than a cookie, but they were always part of our holiday cookie trays, so let's not leave 'em out! Rugelach may look a little fancy, but these treats are anything but divas. If you follow the directions closely, you'll ace them in no time. It all starts with a super tender and flaky cream cheese dough—in fact, we'll use the same cream cheese dough used for Pecan Tassies (page 76). The dough is then rolled out, topped with a filling, cut into tiny wedges, and individually rolled up into croissant-like shapes. Rugelach happily accommodate any sort of fillings from jam and chocolate to dried fruit and nuts. My recent favorite is a mix of dried cranberries, lots of delicious warm spices, and walnuts!

PREP TIME: 30 minutes   **TOTAL TIME:** 3 hours 40 minutes   **YIELD:** 24 cookies

Cream Cheese Dough
3 cups (360 g) all-purpose flour, plus
   more for work surface and rolling out
¼ cup (50 g) granulated sugar
½ teaspoon salt
1 cup (2 sticks, or 240 g) unsalted
   butter, very cold and cubed
8 ounces (227 g) block cream cheese,
   softened to room temperature and
   cut into pieces
1 or 2 teaspoons cold water, if needed

Filling
1 cup (150 g) dried cranberries
1 cup (120 g) chopped walnuts
¾ cup (170 g) packed brown sugar
2 tablespoons (30 g) unsalted butter,
   melted and slightly cooled
2½ teaspoons ground cinnamon
½ teaspoon ground nutmeg
¼ teaspoon ground cloves
¼ teaspoon salt

Topping
1 tablespoon (15 ml) confectioners' sugar,
   for dusting

1. **To make the dough:** Place the flour, granulated sugar, and salt in the bowl of a food processor. Pulse a couple times to blend. Add the cubed butter and cream cheese. Pulse until crumbly; this will take 30 seconds or so. Pulse until there are pea-size crumbs throughout.

2. Pour the dough onto a lightly floured work surface. Fold together with your hands. If the dough seems extremely dry, add 1 teaspoon of cold water on top and mix in. Add up to 1 more teaspoon, if needed.

3. Divide the dough into 3 equal portions, then place each portion onto a large piece of plastic wrap. Wrap each one tightly and pat down to create a disc shape. Chill in the refrigerator for at least 2 hours (and up to 1 day). If chilling for longer than 3 hours, allow the discs to sit at room temperature for at least 30 minutes before rolling and baking.

4. **To make the filling:** Pulse all of the filling ingredients together in a food processor until very finely chopped and well combined. The filling will feel a little moist. You'll have a little over 2 cups (476 g) total.

5. Preheat oven to 350°F (180°C). Line baking sheets with parchment paper or silicone baking mats. Set aside.

6. Remove 1 dough disc from the refrigerator. On a lightly floured work surface, roll into a 10-inch (25 cm) circle (roughly ¼ inch, or 6 mm, thick) and brush the surface lightly with water. Spread about one-third of the filling on top. Gently press the filling down into the dough so it's compact.

continued »

7. Using a pizza cutter or sharp knife, cut the dough into 8 equal wedges. Roll each wedge up, beginning with the wide end and ending with the narrow end. Place the rolls point-side down, 3 inches (7.5 cm) apart, on a baking sheet (see photos, left). Repeat with the remaining 2 discs of dough.

8. Bake the rugelach for 25 to 30 minutes, or until lightly golden brown. As the rugelach bake, the fat in the crust may slightly seep out, giving each a super crunchy crust. This is a good thing!

9. Remove from the oven and allow to cool on baking sheets for 10 minutes before transferring to a wire rack to cool completely. Once cooled, dust lightly with confectioners' sugar.

10. Cookies will stay fresh in an airtight container at room temperature for 4 days or in the refrigerator for up to 1 week.

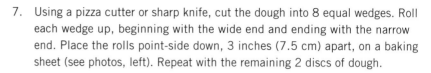

SALLY SAYS

A food processor is imperative for grinding up the filling into one cohesive and moist dough-like consistency. While you can use a pastry cutter to make the dough (see Sally Says *on page 78), I recommend using a food processor because you'll need one anyway for the filling. Do NOT use an electric handheld or stand mixer for this dough.*

Easy Cinnamon Snowballs

When I posted a snowball cookie on my blog a couple of years ago, I loved reading all the names folks have for these cookies in the comments section! Russian tea cakes, Noel balls, Italian wedding cookies, butterballs, snowdrops . . . . While they may have a bajillion different names, one thing remains constant: these buttery and crumbly confections are downright delectable. In this version, I left out the traditional nuts and added cinnamon. And, you only need six basic ingredients.

PREP TIME: 25 minutes **TOTAL TIME:** 1 hour 30 minutes **YIELD:** 32 to 36 cookies

1 cup (2 sticks, or 240 g) unsalted butter, softened to room temperature
2 cups (240 g) confectioners' sugar, divided
1 teaspoon pure vanilla extract
2¼ (270 g) cups all-purpose flour
½ teaspoon salt
1½ teaspoons ground cinnamon, divided

MAKE-AHEAD TIP

See page 12.

Sally Says

For a more traditional version, you can skip the cinnamon and mix 1 cup (110 g) of finely chopped pecans into the dough instead.

1. In a large bowl, using a handheld mixer or a stand mixer fitted with a paddle attachment, beat the butter on medium-high speed until smooth, about 1 minute. Add ¾ cup (90 g) of the confectioners' sugar and the vanilla extract, and beat on medium-high speed until combined and creamy, about 2 minutes. Scrape down the sides and up the bottom of the bowl and beat again as needed to combine.

2. Switch the mixer to low speed and slowly add the flour, ¼ cup (30 g) at a time. Once all of the flour has been added, add the salt and ½ teaspoon of the ground cinnamon. Turn the mixer up to high speed and beat until the dough comes together.

3. Cover and chill the dough in the refrigerator for at least 30 minutes (and up to 4 days). If chilling for longer than 3 hours, allow it to sit at room temperature for at least 30 minutes before rolling and baking.

4. Preheat oven to 350°F (180°C). Line baking sheets with parchment paper or silicone baking mats. Set aside.

5. Roll balls of dough, about 1 tablespoon of dough per cookie, and place 2 inches (5 cm) apart on the baking sheets. Bake the cookies until browned on the bottom edges and just barely browned on top, about 15 minutes.

6. Allow the cookies to cool for 5 minutes on the baking sheets. Mix the remaining 1¼ cups (150 g) confectioners' sugar and 1 teaspoon cinnamon together in a shallow bowl. Gently roll the warm cookies in the mixture to coat completely. Do not discard extra mixture.

7. Place the cookies on wire racks to cool completely. Once completely cooled, roll the cookies in remaining confectioners' sugar–cinnamon mixture again. This is when the sugar will really stick!

8. Cookies will stay fresh in an airtight container at room temperature for up to 1 week.

Shortbread and Slice-and-Bakes Galore

When I find a piece of clothing I adore, I buy it in every single color. I have the same long cardigan in every color available. I've got three pairs of the same boots—black, gray, and brown—and three pairs of the same jeans in every wash available. Likewise, when I find a dependable cookie recipe, I modify it to produce multiple variations.

My basic shortbread recipe is on page 86 (Buttery Shortbread). There's nothing over-the-top about it, really. No dips in chocolate, no snazzy spices, no glamorous additions. But after that recipe, you'll see many variations. And, yes, those include dips in chocolate, snazzy spices, and glamorous additions! Basic shortbread is the most wonderful and dependable blank slate, and after tasting the creations on these first few pages, you'll happily agree—cookie in hand!

The last portion of the chapter is dedicated to my slice-and-bake cookie obsession. My love for slice-and-bake cookies, like my entire rainbow of the same long cardigan sweater, is borderline crazy. Slice-and-bake cookies are, by far, one of the most fun types to make. Like a basic shortbread cookie, they're a fantastic starting point for different flavors. You make the dough, shape it into logs, and chill it in the refrigerator. Then you can roll the logs into a crunchy sugar, finely chopped nuts, or even sprinkles. Then slice off the cookies one by one!

BUTTERY SHORTBREAD

Pure and simple, these shortbread cookies are soft and smooth with crisp edges, making them the perfect complement to a cup of coffee or tea. They're not overly sweet in the slightest. And the best part: you only need five ingredients.

PREP TIME: 20 minutes　　**TOTAL TIME:** 45 minutes　　**YIELD:** 50 (2-inch, or 5 cm) cookies

1½ cups (3 sticks, or 360 g) unsalted butter, softened to room temperature
1 cup (120 g) confectioners' sugar
1 teaspoon pure vanilla extract
2¾ cups (330 g) all-purpose flour, plus more for work surface and rolling out
½ teaspoon salt
1 to 2 teaspoons water, if needed

SALLY SAYS

You can cut the shortbread dough into any shapes. Last year, my friend tested this recipe and cut them into Christmas trees and hearts. Squares, stars . . . anything goes. I used a 2-inch (5 cm) round cookie cutter. For the Chai Tea Spice Shortbread (page 89), I used a tea bag–shaped cookie cutter!

1. Preheat oven to 350°F (180°C). Line baking sheets with parchment paper or silicone baking mats. Set aside.

2. In a large bowl, using a handheld mixer or a stand mixer fitted with a paddle attachment, beat the butter on medium-high speed until smooth, about 1 minute. Add the confectioners' sugar and vanilla extract, and beat on medium-high speed until combined and creamy, about 2 minutes. Scrape down the sides and up the bottom of the bowl and beat again as needed to combine.

3. Switch the mixer to low speed and slowly add the flour, ¼ cup (30 g) at a time. Once all of the flour is incorporated, add the salt. Turn the mixer up to high speed and beat until the dough comes together. Continue beating the dough until it becomes smooth. If the dough is still not smooth after 2 full minutes of beating, add 1 to 2 teaspoons of water.

4. Turn the dough out onto a lightly floured work surface. Divide into 2 equal portions. Using a rolling pin, roll out one portion to ¼ inch (6 mm) thickness. Cut into shapes using a cookie cutter. Reroll the remainder of that portion and continue cutting until all is used. Repeat with the second portion of dough. Place the cookies 3 inches (7.5 cm) apart on the prepared baking sheets.

5. Bake the cookies until very lightly browned on the edges, 12 to 14 minutes. Remove from the oven and allow to cool on baking sheets for 5 minutes before transferring to a wire rack to cool completely.

6. Cookies will stay fresh in an airtight container at room temperature for up to 1 week.

MAKE-AHEAD TIP

You can make the shortbread dough and chill it in the refrigerator for up to 3 days; before using, allow to come to room temperature, then continue with step 4. Another option is to freeze the dough for up to 3 months; thaw overnight in the refrigerator and bring to room temperature before continuing with step 4. Baked cookies freeze well for up to 3 months; thaw overnight in the refrigerator and, if desired, bring to room temperature before serving.

Chai Tea Spice Shortbread

For shortbread with a little more pizzazz, try adding chai spices and dunking into the chocolate. These cookies are not too sweet, and they hit the spot with a steamy chai latte. Of course, you can use any shape of cookie cutter, but one shaped like a tea bag fits the bill!

PREP TIME: 30 minutes   **TOTAL TIME:** 1 hour 15 minutes   **YIELD:** 50 (2-inch, or 5 cm) cookies

1½ cups (3 sticks, or 360 g) unsalted butter, softened to room temperature

1 cup (120 g) confectioners' sugar

1 teaspoon pure vanilla extract

2¾ cups (330 g) all-purpose flour, plus more for work surface and rolling out

1 teaspoon ground cinnamon

½ teaspoon ground allspice

½ teaspoon ground cardamom

½ teaspoon ground cloves

½ teaspoon ground ginger

¼ teaspoon salt

1 to 2 teaspoons water

4-ounce (113 g) bar semi-sweet chocolate, coarsely chopped (optional)

MAKE-AHEAD TIP

See Buttery Shortbread (page 86).

1. Preheat oven to 350°F (180°C). Line baking sheets with parchment paper or silicone baking mats. Set aside.

2. In a large bowl, using a handheld mixer or a stand mixer fitted with a paddle attachment, beat the butter on medium-high speed until smooth, about 1 minute. Add the confectioners' sugar and vanilla extract, and beat on medium-high speed until combined and creamy, about 2 minutes. Scrape down the sides and up the bottom of the bowl and beat again as needed to combine.

3. Switch the mixer to low speed and slowly add the flour, ¼ cup (30 g) at a time. Once all of the flour is incorporated, add the cinnamon, allspice, cardamom, cloves, ginger, and salt. Turn the mixer up to high speed and beat until the dough comes together. Continue beating the dough until it becomes smooth. If the dough is still not smooth after 2 full minutes of beating, add 1 to 2 teaspoons of water.

4. Turn the dough out onto a lightly floured work surface. Divide into 2 equal portions. Roll out one portion to ¼ inch (6 mm) thickness. Cut into shapes using a cookie cutter. Reroll the remainder of that portion and continue cutting until all is used. Repeat with the second portion of dough. Place the cookies 3 inches (7.5 cm) apart on the baking sheets.

5. Bake the cookies until very lightly browned on the edges, 12 to 14 minutes. Remove from the oven and allow to cool on baking sheets for 5 minutes before transferring to a wire rack to cool completely.

6. If dipping in chocolate, once the cookies have cooled completely, melt the chopped chocolate in a double boiler or in the microwave in 15-second increments, stopping and stirring after each until completely smooth. Dip a quarter of each cookie into the chocolate. Allow the chocolate to set completely, about 30 minutes.

7. Cookies will stay fresh in an airtight container at room temperature or in the refrigerator for up to 1 week.

Coconut Lime Shortbread

Reminiscent of a day at the beach, these super buttery and white chocolate–dipped cookies taste like paradise. The recipe is based on that for my Buttery Shortbread (page 86), an excellent starting point for an array of different flavors.

PREP TIME: 30 minutes   **TOTAL TIME:** 1 hours 15 minutes   **YIELD:** 50 (2-inch, or 5 cm) cookies

1½ cups (3 sticks, or 360 g) unsalted butter, softened to room temperature

1 cup (100 g) confectioners' sugar

1 teaspoon pure vanilla extract

1 teaspoon coconut extract

2¾ cups (330 g) all-purpose flour, plus more for work surface and rolling out

¼ teaspoon salt

2 tablespoons (10 g) lime zest

½ cup (45 g) shredded sweetened coconut

1 to 2 teaspoons water

2 (4 ounces, or 113 g, each) bars white chocolate, coarsely chopped

MAKE-AHEAD TIP

See Buttery Shortbread (page 86).

1. Preheat oven to 350°F (180°C). Line baking sheets with parchment paper or silicone baking mats. Set aside.

2. In a large bowl, using a handheld mixer or a stand mixer fitted with a paddle attachment, beat the butter on medium-high speed until smooth, about 1 minute. Add the confectioners' sugar, vanilla extract, and coconut extract, and beat on medium-high speed until combined and creamy, about 2 minutes. Scrape down the sides and up the bottom of the bowl and beat again as needed to combine.

3. Switch the mixer to low speed and slowly add the flour, ¼ cup (30 g) at a time. Once all of the flour is incorporated, add the salt, lime zest, and shredded coconut. Turn the mixer up to high speed and beat until the dough comes together. Continue beating the dough until it becomes smooth. If the dough is still not smooth after 2 full minutes of beating, add 1 to 2 teaspoons of water.

4. Turn the dough out onto a lightly floured work surface. Divide into 2 equal portions. Roll out one portion to ¼ inch (6 mm) thickness. Cut into shapes using a cookie cutter. Reroll the remainder of that portion and continue cutting until all is used. Repeat with the second portion of dough. Place the cookies 3 inches (7.5 cm) apart on the baking sheets.

5. Bake the cookies until very lightly browned on the edges, 12 to 14 minutes. Remove from the oven and allow to cool on baking sheets for 5 minutes before transferring to a wire rack to cool completely.

6. Once the cookies have cooled completely, melt the chopped white chocolate in a double boiler or in the microwave in 15-second increments, stopping and stirring after each until completely smooth. Dip each cookie halfway into the white chocolate. Allow to set completely, about 30 minutes.

7. Cookies will stay fresh in an airtight container at room temperature or in the refrigerator for up to 1 week.

Coffee Toffee Shortbread

The only thing more fun than taking your first bite of these mega-flavorful cookies is saying the rhyming name three times in a row.

PREP TIME: 15 minutes   **TOTAL TIME:** 1 hour 35 minutes   **YIELD:** 50 (2-inch, or 5 cm) cookies

1½ cups (3 sticks, or 360 g) unsalted butter, softened to room temperature

1 cup (120 g) confectioners' sugar

1 teaspoon pure vanilla extract

2¾ cups (330 g) all-purpose flour, plus more for work surface and rolling out

2 teaspoons espresso powder

¼ teaspoon salt

1 cup plus 2 tablespoons (270 g) toffee bits (such as Heath Bits 'o Brickle Toffee Bits)

1 to 2 teaspoons water

2 (4 ounces, or 113 g, each) bars milk chocolate, coarsely chopped

- handheld or stand mixer fitted with a paddle attachment
- rolling pin
- cookie cutter

MAKE-AHEAD TIP

See Buttery Shortbread (page 86).

SALLY SAYS

See Sally Says on page 192.

1. Preheat oven to 350°F (180°C). Line baking sheets with parchment paper or silicone baking mats. Set aside.

2. In a large bowl, using a handheld mixer or a stand mixer fitted with a paddle attachment, beat the butter on medium-high speed until smooth, about 1 minute. Add the confectioners' sugar and vanilla extract, and beat on medium-high speed until combined and creamy, about 2 minutes. Scrape down the sides and up the bottom of the bowl and beat again as needed to combine.

3. Switch the mixer to low speed and slowly add the flour, ¼ cup (30 g) at a time. Once all of the flour is incorporated, add the espresso powder, salt, and toffee bits. Turn the mixer up to high speed and beat until the dough comes together. Continue beating the dough until it becomes smooth. If the dough is still not smooth after 2 full minutes of beating, add 1 to 2 teaspoons of water.

4. Turn the dough out onto a lightly floured work surface. Divide into 2 equal portions. Roll out one portion to ¼ inch (6 mm) thickness. Cut into shapes using a cookie cutter. Reroll the remainder of that portion and continue cutting until all is used. Repeat with the second portion of dough. Place the cookies 3 inches (7.5 cm) apart on the baking sheets.

5. Bake the cookies until very lightly browned on the edges, 12 to 14 minutes. The toffee will bubble on the sides and tops. This is okay! Remove from the oven and allow to cool on baking sheets for 5 minutes before transferring to a wire rack to cool completely.

6. Once the cookies have cooled completely, melt the chopped chocolate in a double boiler or in the microwave in 15-second increments, stopping and stirring after each until completely smooth. Dip each cookie halfway into the chocolate. Allow the chocolate to set completely, about 30 minutes.

7. Cookies will stay fresh in an airtight container at room temperature or in the refrigerator for up to 1 week.

Shortbread Jam Thumbprints

These are the sparkling jewels of the cookie world. Fill with whatever you like best, but I prefer either lemon curd or a mix of jams (see *Sally Says*, below, if you want to make yours with lemon curd). This is just the beginning of thumbprint madness, so get your thumbs ready!

PREP TIME: 15 minutes   **TOTAL TIME:** 1 hour 35 minutes   **YIELD:** 36 cookies

¾ cup (1½ sticks, or 180 g) unsalted butter, softened to room temperature

½ cup (60 g) confectioners' sugar

1 teaspoon pure vanilla extract

½ teaspoon almond extract

1½ cups (180 g) all-purpose flour

¼ teaspoon salt

⅓ cup (35 g) finely crushed pecans

6 tablespoons (120 g) favorite jam or jelly

Sally Says

If you're using lemon curd, spoon the filling into the thumbprints halfway through baking. (You'll need 6 tablespoons, or 110 g, of lemon curd.) Bake the cookies for 6 minutes in step 5, remove from the oven, fill each with ½ teaspoon of lemon curd, and continue baking for 6 to 7 more minutes. For extra lemon flavor, add 1 tablespoon (5 g) of lemon zest to the dough. I didn't coat the lemon curd thumbprints in the photo with pecans, but you can.

1. In a large bowl, using a handheld mixer or a stand mixer fitted with a paddle attachment, beat the butter on medium-high speed until smooth, about 1 minute. Add the confectioners' sugar, vanilla extract, and almond extract, and beat on medium-high speed until combined and creamy, about 2 minutes. Scrape down the sides and up the bottom of the bowl and beat again as needed to combine.

2. Switch the mixer to low speed and slowly add the flour, ¼ cup (30 g) at a time. Once all of the flour is incorporated, add the salt. Turn the mixer up to high speed and beat until the dough comes together. Continue beating the dough until it becomes smooth.

3. Roll the dough into balls, 2 teaspoons of dough per cookie, then roll each ball into the crushed pecans. Press your thumb or the handle tip of a rubber spatula or wooden spoon into the center of each dough ball to make an indentation. Place the unbaked cookies on 1 or 2 large plates. Cover loosely and refrigerate for 1 hour (and up to 2 days).

4. Preheat oven to 350°F (180°C). Line baking sheets with parchment paper or silicone baking mats.

5. Remove unbaked cookies from the refrigerator and spoon ½ teaspoon of jam into each indentation. Arrange cookies 3 inches (7.5 cm) apart on the baking sheets. Bake for 12 to 13 minutes, or until lightly browned on the sides. The jam won't look completely set, but it will set as the cookies cool.

6. Remove from the oven. Allow the cookies to cool on the baking sheets for 5 minutes before transferring to a wire rack to cool completely.

7. Cookies will stay fresh in an airtight container at room temperature for 2 days or in the refrigerator for up to 1 week.

MAKE-AHEAD TIP

Make the dough through step 3 and chill it in the refrigerator for up to 2 days. Or prepare the dough only through step 2 and freeze it for up to 3 months; for the latter, thaw the dough overnight in the refrigerator, then bring to room temperature and continue with step 3. Baked cookies, with filling, freeze well for up to 3 months; thaw overnight in the refrigerator and, if desired, bring to room temperature before serving.

Chocolate Cashew Shortbread Wedges

I made similar shortbread wedges during the holidays last year. They're easy, with absolutely no dough chilling required. All you need are an electric mixer, a couple of round cake pans, and some basic ingredients. Think of these as cookie pizza wedges—with chocolate on top!

PREP TIME: 20 minutes   **TOTAL TIME:** 2 hours 30 minutes   **YIELD:** 24 cookies

1 cup (2 sticks, or 240 g) unsalted butter, softened to room temperature

½ cup (100 g) granulated sugar

¼ cup (60 g) packed light brown sugar

1 teaspoon pure vanilla extract

1 teaspoon salt

2¼ (270 g) cups all-purpose flour

1¼ cups (160 g) chopped salted cashews, divided

4-ounce (113 g) bar semi-sweet or bittersweet chocolate, coarsely chopped

coarse sea salt, for topping

1. Preheat oven to 325°F (170°C). Line two 9-inch (23 cm) cake pans with parchment paper, leaving enough overhang around the edge of each to easily lift out the shortbread. (I encourage using parchment so that you can easily remove the shortbread and not cut it while it's in the pan.

2. In a large bowl, using a handheld mixer or a stand mixer fitted with a paddle attachment, beat the butter on medium-high speed until smooth, about 1 minute. Add the granulated sugar and brown sugar, and beat on medium-high speed until creamed, about 2 minutes. Scrape down the sides and up the bottom of the bowl and beat again as needed to combine.

3. Add the vanilla extract, salt, and flour, and beat on low speed, gradually increasing to high speed as the mixture combines. Add 1 cup (130 g) of the cashews, reserving the rest for sprinkling on top of the wedges. Turn the mixer up to high speed and beat until the dough comes together.

4. Press half of the dough evenly into each of the prepared cake pans. Make sure the dough is compact in the pan. Bake for 30 minutes, or until lightly browned on top and around the edges.

5. Remove from the oven and allow to cool for 10 minutes. Carefully remove the shortbread from the pans by lifting the overhanging parchment paper (see photo, left). Cut the shortbread in each pan into 12 wedges. You want to make sure to do this while the shortbread is still warm. Allow to cool completely on the parchment.

6. Melt the chopped chocolate in a double boiler or in the microwave in 15-second increments, stopping and stirring after each until completely smooth. Drizzle over the cooled shortbread wedges and sprinkle with the remaining ¼ cup (30 g) chopped cashews and sea salt. Allow the chocolate to set completely, about 20 minutes.

7. Shortbread will stay fresh in an airtight container at room temperature for up to 5 days or in the refrigerator for up to 1 week.

MAKE-AHEAD TIP

You can make the shortbread dough and chill it in the refrigerator for up to
3 days; before using, allow it to come to room temperature and then continue with
step 4. Unbaked shortbread dough freezes well for up to 3 months; allow to thaw
overnight in the refrigerator, then bring to room temperature before continuing with
step 4. Baked shortbread freezes well for up to 3 months; thaw overnight in the
refrigerator and, if desired, bring to room temperature before serving.

Jam Shortbread Bars

These shortbread bars come to life with just six ordinary ingredients. We skip rolling and shaping by simply pressing the dough into a baking pan and covering with jam. Have fun testing out different jam flavors. You might even use different flavors of jam for each half of the shortbread!

PREP TIME: 15 minutes   **TOTAL TIME:** 4 hours   **YIELD:** 24 bars

2 cups (4 sticks, or 480 g) unsalted butter, softened to room temperature
4 cups (480 g) all-purpose flour
1 cup (120 g) confectioners' sugar, plus more for dusting
2 teaspoons pure vanilla extract
½ teaspoon salt
1 cup (320 g) favorite jam or jelly

Sally Says

Depending on which flavor of jam you use, you might try adding ½ teaspoon of almond extract to the dough when you add the vanilla extract. Almond extract pairs deliciously with peach, raspberry, and/or strawberry.

1. Preheat oven to 350°F (180°C). Line a 9 × 13-inch (23 × 33 cm) baking pan with parchment paper, leaving enough overhang around the edges to easily lift out the shortbread. (I encourage using parchment so that you can easily remove the shortbread and not cut it while it's in the pan.)

2. In a large bowl, using a handheld mixer or a stand mixer fitted with a paddle attachment, beat the butter on medium-high speed until smooth, about 2 minutes. Add the flour and confectioners' sugar, and beat on low speed for a few seconds, then gradually work up to medium-high speed. Beat on medium-high speed until combined and creamy, about 2 minutes. Scrape down the sides and up the bottom of the bowl and beat again as needed to combine. Beat in the vanilla extract and salt.

3. Press the dough evenly into the prepared baking pan, saving ¾ cup (168 g) of dough for crumbling on top.

4. Bake for 15 minutes. Remove pan from the oven and carefully spread the jam on top of the shortbread. The warmth of the dough will help distribute the jam. Crumble the reserved dough and sprinkle on top of the jam. Return the shortbread to the oven and bake for 30 minutes, or until jam appears set on top.

5. Remove from the oven and allow the shortbread to cool completely in the pan set on a wire rack. Once completely cool, about 3 hours, remove the shortbread from the pan by picking it up with the parchment paper overhanging the sides. Lightly dust the top of the shortbread with confectioners' sugar. Cut into squares. Note: If shortbread is not completely cool, the bars will fall apart when cutting.

6. Bars will stay fresh in an airtight container at room temperature for up to 5 days or in the refrigerator for up to 1 week.

MAKE-AHEAD TIP

Prepare the dough as described in step 2. Cover tightly and refrigerate for up to 3 days or freeze for up to 3 months. Before using, allow dough to come to room temperature (thawing overnight first, if frozen); preheat the oven, prepare the baking pan as described in step 1, and then continue on to step 3. Baked bars can be frozen for up to 3 months, but if you decide to do this, hold off dusting the top with confectioners' sugar; allow bars to thaw overnight in the refrigerator, then dust with confectioners' sugar right before serving.

Maple Walnut Slice-and-Bake Cookies

I tested this maple cookie recipe a few times before the holidays last year. I brought two batches to a party, and my friends asked me—no, BEGGED me—for the recipe. The maple flavor is front and center, complemented by the cinnamon and walnuts. Instead of maple syrup, I suggest using super-potent maple extract, found in most major grocery stores. And you'll smell that maple a mile away!

PREP TIME: 25 minutes   **TOTAL TIME:** 6 hours 10 minutes   **YIELD:** 24 cookies

2 cups (240 g) all-purpose flour, plus more for work surface and hands

½ teaspoon ground cinnamon

¼ teaspoon salt

¾ cup (1½ sticks, or 180 g) unsalted butter, softened to room temperature

⅔ cup (150 g) packed dark brown sugar

1 large egg, room temperature

1½ teaspoons maple extract

1¼ cups (150 g) chopped walnuts, divided

½ cup (60 g) coarse sugar, for rolling

2 (4 ounces, or 113 g, each) bars white chocolate, coarsely chopped

1. Whisk the flour, cinnamon, and salt together in a medium bowl. Set aside.

2. In a large bowl, using a handheld mixer or a stand mixer fitted with a paddle attachment, beat the butter on medium-high speed until smooth, about 1 minute. Add the brown sugar and beat on medium-high speed until creamed, about 2 minutes. Add the egg and maple extract, and beat on high speed until combined, about 1 minute. Scrape down the sides and up the bottom of the bowl and beat again as needed to combine.

3. Add the dry ingredients to the wet ingredients and mix on low speed until combined, then beat in 1 cup (120 g) of the chopped walnuts. The dough will be thick and slightly sticky.

4. Turn the dough out onto a floured work surface and, with floured hands, divide into 2 equal portions. Shape each portion into an 8-inch (20 cm) log, about 2½ inches (6 cm) in diameter. Tightly wrap the logs in plastic wrap (see photo, left) and chill in the refrigerator for at least 4 hours (and up to 5 days). Chilling is important for this dough, to prevent the cookies from spreading in the oven and losing their shape. I prefer to chill it overnight.

5. Preheat oven to 350°F (180°C). Line baking sheets with parchment paper or silicone baking mats. Set aside. Pour coarse sugar onto a large plate.

6. Remove the logs from refrigerator and roll them in the coarse sugar (see photo, opposite). Slice each log into 12 equally thick cookies and place the cookies on the baking sheets about 2 inches (5 cm) apart. Bake the cookies for 12 to 14 minutes, or until brown around the edges.

7. Remove from the oven and allow to cool on the baking sheets for 5 minutes before transferring to a wire rack to cool completely.

8. Melt the chopped white chocolate in a double boiler or in the microwave in 15-second increments, stopping and stirring after each until completely smooth. Dip each cookie halfway into the white chocolate. Sprinkle remaining ¼ cup (30 g) chopped walnuts on top of the dipped part of the cookies. Allow the white chocolate to set completely, about 30 minutes.

9. Cookies will stay fresh in an airtight container at room temperature or in the refrigerator for up to 1 week.

MAKE-AHEAD TIP

Baked slice-and-bake cookies, without any chocolate or frosting, freeze well for up to 3 months; allow cookies to thaw overnight in the refrigerator, then bring to room temperature before dipping in chocolate or frosting and serving. Cookie dough logs freeze well, too, for up to 3 months; allow the logs to thaw overnight in the refrigerator, then continue with step 6.

Vanilla Spice Slice-and-Bake Cookies

Like the other slice-and-bake recipes in this chapter, these frosted cookies have a unique texture. They're soft in the center with a crumbly crisp edge. You can't stop at one!

PREP TIME: 25 minutes **TOTAL TIME:** 5 hours **YIELD:** 24 cookies

2 cups (240 g) all-purpose flour, plus more for work surface and hands
½ teaspoon ground cinnamon
¼ teaspoon ground nutmeg
¼ teaspoon salt
¾ cup (1½ sticks, or 180 g) unsalted butter, softened to room temperature
⅔ cup (150 g) packed light brown sugar
1 large egg, room temperature
2 teaspoons pure vanilla extract
seeds scraped from ½ vanilla bean
½ cup (60 g) coarse sugar, for rolling
Vanilla Frosting (page 13)
sprinkles, for decorating (optional)

MAKE-AHEAD TIP

See Maple Walnut Slice-and-Bake Cookies (page 100).

Sally Says

I like to roll the logs in coarse sugar (step 6). The kind I typically use is Sugar In The Raw® Turbinado Cane Sugar. However, I used Wilton® White Sparkling Sugar for these.

1. Whisk the flour, cinnamon, nutmeg, and salt together in a medium bowl. Set aside.

2. In a large bowl, using a handheld mixer or a stand mixer fitted with a paddle attachment, beat the butter on medium-high speed until smooth, about 1 minute. Add the brown sugar and beat on medium-high speed until creamed, about 2 minutes. Add the egg, vanilla extract, and vanilla seeds, and beat on high speed until combined, about 1 minute. Scrape down the sides and up the bottom of the bowl and beat again as needed to combine.

3. Add the dry ingredients to the wet ingredients and mix on low speed until combined. The dough will be thick and slightly sticky.

4. Turn the dough out onto a floured work surface and, with floured hands, divide into 2 equal portions. Shape each portion into an 8-inch (20 cm) log, about 2½ inches (6 cm) in diameter. Tightly wrap the logs in plastic wrap and chill in the refrigerator for at least 4 hours (and up to 5 days). Chilling is important for this dough, to prevent the cookies from spreading in the oven and losing their shape. I prefer to chill it overnight.

5. Preheat oven to 350°F (180°C). Line baking sheets with parchment paper or silicone baking mats. Set aside. Pour coarse sugar onto a large plate.

6. Remove the logs from refrigerator and roll them in coarse sugar. Slice each log into 12 equally thick cookies and place the cookies on the baking sheets about 2 inches (5 cm) apart. Bake the cookies for 12 to 14 minutes, or until brown around the edges.

7. Remove from the oven and allow to cool on the baking sheets for 5 minutes before transferring to a wire rack to let cool completely before frosting. Once the cookies have cooled completely, spread on Vanilla Frosting and, if desired, decorate with sprinkles.

8. Frosted cookies will stay fresh in an airtight container at room temperature for 2 days or in the refrigerator for up to 1 week.

Mint Chocolate Slice-and-Bake Cookies

And, of course, I have a chocolate version of slice-and-bakes! Think of these as Chocolate Sugar Cookies (page 34) without the rolling pin, royal icing, or cookie cutters. Peppermint extract gives the cookies even more flavor, but they wouldn't be lacking if you didn't have any on hand.

PREP TIME: 25 minutes   **TOTAL TIME:** 5 hours   **YIELD:** 24 cookies

1½ cups (180 g) all-purpose flour, plus more for work surface and hands

¾ cup (65 g) unsweetened natural or Dutch-process cocoa powder

¼ teaspoon salt

¾ cup (1½ sticks, or 180 g) unsalted butter, softened to room temperature

¾ cup (150 g) granulated sugar

¼ cup (60 g) packed brown sugar

1 large egg, room temperature

1 teaspoon pure vanilla extract

1 teaspoon pure peppermint extract

2 (4 ounces, or 113 g, each) bars semi-sweet chocolate, coarsely chopped

MAKE-AHEAD TIP

See Maple Walnut Slice-and-Bake Cookies (page 100).

 ## Sally Says

Make sure to use peppermint extract, as opposed to simply "mint" extract. I find that the latter tastes more like toothpaste than anything else! If you like super-minty flavor, stir ½ teaspoon of peppermint extract into the melted chocolate along with ½ teaspoon of vegetable oil.

1. Whisk the flour, cocoa powder, and salt together in a medium bowl. Set aside.

2. In a large bowl, using a handheld mixer or a stand mixer fitted with a paddle attachment, beat the butter on medium-high speed until smooth, about 1 minute. Add the granulated sugar and brown sugar, and beat on medium-high speed until creamed, about 2 minutes. Add the egg, vanilla extract, and peppermint extract, and beat on high speed until combined, about 1 minute. Scrape down the sides and up the bottom of the bowl and beat again as needed to combine.

3. Add the dry ingredients to the wet ingredients and mix on low speed until combined. The dough will be slightly sticky.

4. Turn the dough out onto a floured work surface and, with floured hands, divide into 2 equal portions. Shape each portion into an 8-inch (20 cm) log, about 2½ inches (6 cm) in diameter. Tightly wrap the logs in plastic wrap and chill in the refrigerator for at least 4 hours (and up to 5 days). Chilling is important for this dough, to prevent the cookies from spreading in the oven and losing their shape. I prefer to chill it overnight.

5. Preheat oven to 350°F (180°C). Line baking sheets with parchment paper or silicone baking mats. Set aside.

6. Remove the logs from refrigerator. Slice each log into 12 equally thick cookies and place the cookies on the baking sheets about 2 inches (5 cm) apart. Bake the cookies for 12 to 13 minutes.

7. Remove from the oven and allow to cool on the baking sheets for 5 minutes before transferring to a wire rack to cool completely.

8. Melt the chopped chocolate in a double boiler or in the microwave in 15-second increments, stopping and stirring after each until completely smooth. Dip each cooled cookie halfway into the chocolate. Allow the chocolate to set completely, about 30 minutes.

9. Cookies will stay fresh in an airtight container at room temperature or in the refrigerator for up to 1 week.

The Sprinkle Chapter

This cookbook is practically bursting with joy. That's simply what you get from a book filled with cookies. However, no chapter compares to what you are about to experience. If a unicorn, a fairy, and My Little Pony owned a bakery together, it would be located under a rainbow. And they'd sell the confections you'll learn to make on the following pages.

And if that thought weren't enough to entice you (seriously, a unicorn rainbow bakery!), this chapter also includes a glossary of sprinkles, my favorite sugar cookie bars, and even a sprinkle-filled cookie pizza!

Welcome to the happiest recipes on earth.

Nonpareils

Quins

Sanding Sugar

Sprinkles

Sprinkle Glossary

Sprinkles—the most colorful of a baker's ingredients—come in many shapes and go by many names. While there are many different types, I'm just going to review the ones used in this cookbook (many of which I get from Sweetapolita's online shop, sweetapolitashop.com). Let's get ready to get creative and dive into this colorful world!

Nonpareils

These are teeny-tiny balls. They're the miniscule sprinkles that you find all over your house and even on your car seat. Just me? Moving on. Nonpareils are great for coating cookies such as Rainbow Kiss Cookies (page 118), but I would steer clear of mixing them into cookie dough, as their color bleeds easily.

Quins

Did you know my married name is Quinn? This may be one of the many reasons I married Kevin. But in all seriousness, quins (also called "confetti" sprinkles) are flat edible adornments, typically circular in shape, though you can find them in the form of hearts, stars, leaves, etc. You can use them as a decorative topping or inside cookie dough. In this chapter, whenever a recipe calls for "sprinkles," you can use quins if you wish.

Sanding Sugar

Resembling coarse sugar, this type of sprinkle comes in a variety of colors and, as you'll see with Sugar Cookie Sparkles (page 110), is wonderful for using to coat cookies. In this chapter, whenever a recipe calls for "sprinkles" you can use sanding sugar if you like.

Sprinkles

Also known as "jimmies" or "toppers" (depending on where you're from), these are the basic, small, cylindrical edible embellishments most often used. They come in an array of single colors, various mixed colors (including rainbow), and even chocolate. They're fantastic for decorating cookies or mixing into cookie dough.

Sugar Cookie Sparkles

I love these sugar cookies—not only are they coated with colorful sparkles, but you don't need a rolling pin to make them. This is a simple drop cookie recipe producing super soft and creamy sugar cookies. My trick to this texture—and feel free to borrow it!—is a little cream cheese.

PREP TIME: 15 minutes   **TOTAL TIME:** 2 hours 5 minutes   **YIELD:** 32 to 34 cookies

3 cups (360 g) all-purpose flour
1½ teaspoons baking powder
½ teaspoon salt
1 cup (2 sticks, or 240 g) unsalted butter, softened to room temperature
2 ounces (56 g) block cream cheese, softened to room temperature
1 cup (200 g) granulated sugar
1 large egg, room temperature
2 teaspoons pure vanilla extract
½ teaspoon almond extract
¾ cup (90 g) sanding sugar, any color or assorted colors

MAKE-AHEAD TIP

See page 12.

1. Whisk the flour, baking powder, and salt together in a medium bowl until combined. Set aside.

2. In a large bowl, using a handheld mixer or a stand mixer fitted with a paddle attachment, beat the butter and cream cheese together on medium-high speed until smooth, about 2 minutes. Add the granulated sugar and beat on medium-high speed until creamed, about 1 minute. Add the egg, vanilla extract, and almond extract, and beat on high speed until combined, about 1 minute. Scrape down the sides and up the bottom of the bowl and beat again as needed to combine.

3. Add the dry ingredients to the wet ingredients and mix on low speed until combined. The dough will be thick.

4. Cover and chill the dough in the refrigerator for 1 hour (and up to 4 days). If chilling for longer than 3 hours, allow it to sit at room temperature for at least 30 minutes before rolling and baking because the dough will be quite hard and the cookies may not spread.

5. Preheat oven to 350°F (180°C). Line baking sheets with parchment paper or silicone baking mats. Set aside.

6. Pour the sanding sugar into a bowl or, if using a few colors, several individual bowls.

7. Roll balls of dough, using 1 tablespoon of dough per cookie, and then roll each ball into the sanding sugar to coat. Place each ball 2 inches (5 cm) apart on the baking sheets.

8. Using the back of a measuring cup or drinking glass, gently press down on each cookie to slightly flatten. Bake the cookies for 12 to 13 minutes, or until very lightly browned on the edges.

9. Remove from the oven and allow to cool on the baking sheets for 5 minutes before transferring the cookies to a wire rack to cool completely.

10. Cookies will stay fresh in an airtight container at room temperature for up to 1 week.

Soft-Baked Sugar Cookie Bars

I had to include sugar cookie bars in this cookbook. Why? They're SO EASY. There's no chilling or rolling. Just flatten the dough into a pan and let the oven do the magic!

PREP TIME: 25 minutes   **TOTAL TIME:** 3 hours   **YIELD:** 24 bars

2¾ cups (330 g) all-purpose flour

1½ teaspoons baking powder

½ teaspoon salt

1 cup (2 sticks, or 240 g) unsalted butter, softened to room temperature

1¼ (250 g) cups granulated sugar

1 large egg plus 1 egg yolk, both at room temperature

2 teaspoons pure vanilla extract

Vanilla Frosting (page 13)

3 drops purple liquid food coloring (optional)

2 tablespoons (20 g) sprinkles

 Sally Says

I like to pipe the frosting onto the bars, as you see in the photo. If you'd like to re-create this look, use the Wilton® #1M piping tip. Working with this piping tip is very easy. All I did here was apply pressure to squeeze the frosting out, and slowly lift straight up.

1. Preheat oven to 350°F (180°C). Line a 9 × 13-inch (23 × 33 cm) baking pan with parchment paper, leaving enough overhang around the sides to easily lift out the baked dough.

2. Whisk the flour, baking powder, and salt together in a medium bowl until combined. Set aside.

3. In a large bowl, using a handheld mixer or a stand mixer fitted with a paddle attachment, beat the butter on medium-high speed until smooth, about 2 minutes. Add the granulated sugar and beat on medium-high speed until creamed, about 1 minute. Add the egg, egg yolk, and vanilla extract, and beat on high speed until combined, about 1 minute. Scrape down the sides and up the bottom of the bowl and beat again as needed to combine.

4. Add the dry ingredients to the wet ingredients and mix on low speed until combined. The dough will be thick.

5. Press the dough evenly into the prepared baking pan. Bake for 20 to 22 minutes, or until the edges are lightly browned.

6. Remove from the oven and allow the baked cookie dough to cool completely in the pan set on a wire rack. Once cool, remove from the pan by lifting the sides of the parchment paper.

7. If desired, add 3 drops of purple food coloring to the Vanilla Frosting, or a couple drops each of red and blue food coloring, to create a purple shade. Frost the baked cookie dough with Vanilla Frosting, top with sprinkles, and cut into squares.

8. Frosted bars will stay fresh in an airtight container at room temperature for up to 2 days or in the refrigerator for up to 1 week.

MAKE-AHEAD TIP

Prepare the dough as described in steps 2 through 4. Cover tightly and refrigerate for up to 3 days or freeze for up to 3 months; allow to thaw overnight in the refrigerator. Before using, allow dough to come to room temperature, preheat the oven, prepare the baking pan as described in step 1, and continue with step 5. Unfrosted baked cut bars can be frozen for up to 3 months; allow to thaw overnight in the refrigerator, then frost before serving.

Birthday Party Thumbprints

There's always that fun, slightly quirky one in a group of girlfriends. She dresses boldly, plans all the parties, cracks all the jokes, smiles brightly, and whenever you're with her, you always have the best time. Consider this recipe the fun and quirky one in the thumbprint cookie gang.

PREP TIME: 15 minutes   **TOTAL TIME:** 1 hour 45 minutes   **YIELD:** 36 cookies

Cookie Dough

¾ cup (1½ sticks, or 180 g) unsalted butter, softened to room temperature
½ cup (60 g) confectioners' sugar
2 teaspoons pure vanilla extract
seeds scraped from ½ vanilla bean
1½ cups (180 g) all-purpose flour
¼ teaspoon salt
⅔ cup (110 g) plus 2 tablespoons (20 g) rainbow sprinkles, divided

White Chocolate Ganache

3 ounces (85 g) white chocolate, coarsely chopped
3 tablespoons (45 ml) heavy cream
1 very small drop red or pink liquid food coloring (optional)

MAKE-AHEAD TIP

Make the cookie dough through step 3 and chill in the refrigerator for up to 2 days. You can also freeze unbaked cookie dough for up to 3 months. If you opt for the latter, prepare the dough only through step 2 (in other words, don't roll the dough into individual balls); thaw overnight in the refrigerator, then bring to room temperature and continue with step 3. Baked cookies, with ganache filling, freeze well for up to 3 months; thaw overnight in the refrigerator and bring to room temperature, if desired, before serving.

1. **To make the dough:** In a large bowl, using a handheld mixer or a stand mixer fitted with a paddle attachment, beat the butter on medium-high speed until smooth, about 1 minute. Add the confectioners' sugar, vanilla extract, and vanilla seeds, and beat on medium-high speed until combined and creamy, about 2 minutes. Scrape down the sides and up the bottom of the bowl and beat again as needed to combine.

2. Switch the mixer to low speed and slowly add the flour, ¼ cup (30 g) at a time. Once all of the flour is incorporated, add the salt. Turn the mixer up to high speed and beat until the dough comes together. Continue beating the dough until it becomes smooth. Once smooth, beat in ⅔ cup (110 g) of the sprinkles on low speed.

3. Roll balls of dough, 2 teaspoons of dough per cookie. Press your thumb or the handle tip of a rubber spatula or wooden spoon into the center of each dough ball to make an indentation. Place the unbaked cookies on 1 or 2 large plates. Cover loosely and refrigerate for 1 hour (and up to 2 days).

4. Preheat oven to 350°F (180°C). Line baking sheets with parchment paper or silicone baking mats.

5. Remove unbaked cookies from the refrigerator and arrange 3 inches (7.5 cm) apart on the baking sheets. Bake for 12 to 13 minutes, or until lightly browned on the sides.

6. Remove from the oven. If the indentations have puffed up, press the handle tip of a rubber spatula or wooden spoon into the cookies again. Allow the cookies to cool on the baking sheets for 5 minutes before transferring to a wire rack to cool completely.

7. **To make the ganache:** Place the chopped white chocolate in a small heatproof bowl. Heat the cream in a small saucepan over medium heat, stirring occasionally. Once the cream begins to boil, immediately remove it from the heat and pour it over the white chocolate. Stir gently and slowly until the ganache is smooth. If desired, stir in food coloring to obtain a pink color. Allow ganache to cool for 10 minutes before spooning into cookies. During this time, it will slowly thicken.

8. Once ganache is ready, spoon ½ teaspoon in each cooled cookie, or however much fills each. Top with remaining 2 tablespoons (20 g) sprinkles. Enjoy the cookies right away or wait until ganache is relatively set, about 2 hours.

9. Cookies will stay fresh in an airtight container at room temperature for 2 days or in the refrigerator for up to 1 week.

Soft Funfetti Chip Cookies

On my blog, I have a recipe for cookies that are so festive, they actually appear on the cover of my first cookbook, *Sally's Baking Addiction*. That particular recipe uses cake mix in addition to flour to create a birthday cake flavor. However, I wanted to create a version that didn't include cake mix. While these soft cookies don't have the exact same flavor, they're every bit as celebration-worthy and delicious!

PREP TIME: 30 minutes   **TOTAL TIME:** 2 hours 30 minutes   **YIELD:** 36 cookies

2½ (300 g) cups all-purpose flour

2 teaspoons cornstarch

1 teaspoon baking soda

½ teaspoon salt

1 cup (2 sticks, or 240 g) unsalted butter, softened to room temperature

1 cup (225 g) packed brown sugar

½ cup (100 g) granulated sugar

2 large eggs, room temperature

2 teaspoons pure vanilla extract

1½ cups (270 g) semi-sweet chocolate chips

⅔ cup (110 g) sprinkles

MAKE-AHEAD TIP

See page 12.

1. Whisk the flour, cornstarch, baking soda, and salt together in a medium bowl. Set aside.

2. In a large bowl, using a handheld mixer or a stand mixer fitted with a paddle attachment, beat the butter on medium-high speed until smooth, about 1 minute. Add the brown sugar and granulated sugar, and beat on medium-high speed until creamed, about 2 minutes. Add the eggs and vanilla extract, and beat on high speed until combined, about 1 minute. Scrape down the sides and up the bottom of the bowl and beat again as needed to combine.

3. Add the dry ingredients to the wet ingredients and mix on low speed until combined. With the mixer running on low speed, add the chocolate chips and sprinkles. The dough will be soft and thick. Cover and chill the dough for at least 1½ hours (and up to 4 days). If chilling for longer than 3 hours, allow it to sit at room temperature for at least 30 minutes before rolling and baking because the dough will be quite hard.

4. Preheat oven to 350°F (180°C). Line baking sheets with parchment paper or silicone baking mats. Set aside.

5. Roll balls of dough, about 1½ tablespoons of dough per cookie, and place 3 inches (7.5 cm) apart on the baking sheets. Bake for 12 to 13 minutes, or until lightly browned on the sides. The centers will look very soft.

6. Remove from the oven and allow to cool on the baking sheets for 5 minutes before transferring to a wire rack to cool completely. While the cookies are still warm, I like to press a few more chocolate chips into the tops—this is only for looks!

7. Cookies will stay fresh in an airtight container at room temperature for up to 1 week.

Rainbow Kiss Cookies

So much joy in one tiny chocolate cookie! I like making Rainbow Kiss Cookies for Valentine's Day . . . decadent chocolate and happy sprinkles with a kiss on top!

PREP TIME: 15 minutes   **TOTAL TIME:** 1 hour   **YIELD:** 36 cookies

1 cup (120 g) all-purpose flour
½ cup (43 g) unsweetened natural or Dutch-process cocoa powder
¼ teaspoon salt
½ cup (1 stick, or 120 g) unsalted butter, softened to room temperature
⅔ cup (130 g) granulated sugar
1 egg yolk, room temperature
2 tablespoons (30 ml) milk
1 teaspoon pure vanilla extract
¾ cup (120 g) rainbow nonpareil sprinkles
36 chocolate Hershey's Kisses®, unwrapped

MAKE-AHEAD TIP

See page 12.

 SALLY SAYS
Why no baking soda or baking powder? To keep these cookies compact and dense so that they hold their shape around the Hershey's Kiss®, skip the leavening agents.

1. Preheat oven to 350°F (180°C). Line baking sheets with parchment paper or silicone baking mats. Set aside.

2. Whisk the flour, cocoa powder, and salt together in a medium bowl. Set aside.

3. In a large bowl, using a handheld mixer or a stand mixer fitted with a paddle attachment, beat the butter on medium-high speed until smooth, about 1 minute. Add the granulated sugar and beat on medium-high speed until creamed, about 2 minutes. Add the egg yolk, milk, and vanilla extract, and beat on high speed until combined, about 1 minute. Scrape down the sides and up the bottom of the bowl and beat again as needed to combine.

4. Add the dry ingredients to the wet ingredients and mix on low speed until combined.

5. Pour the sprinkles into a small bowl. Roll balls of dough, 2 teaspoons of dough per cookie, then roll each ball into the sprinkles to coat. Place dough balls 2 inches (5 cm) apart on the baking sheets.

6. Bake the cookies for 10 to 12 minutes.

7. Remove from the oven. Allow to cool on the baking sheets for 5 minutes, then press a chocolate Hershey's Kiss® into the center of each cookie. Transfer the cookies to a wire rack to cool completely.

8. Cookies will stay fresh in an airtight container at room temperature for up to 1 week.

Fairy Meringues

Just like a teeny-tiny fairy, these magical, sprinkled meringue cookies are light as air! If this is your first time making meringue cookies, you'll be happy to know there are very few ingredients required. Cream of tartar is key for stabilizing the egg whites, but hopefully you already picked up a bottle for making Brown Butter Snickerdoodles (page 18). Most of the work is done in the oven, where the whipped meringue dries out into a delightful crisp and melt-in-your-mouth texture. The unique thing about meringue cookies is that they are baked at a low temperature for a long period of time.

PREP TIME: 20 minutes   **TOTAL TIME:** 3 hours 30 minutes   **YIELD:** 32 (1½-inch, or 4 cm) cookies

3 large egg whites, room temperature
⅛ teaspoon cream of tartar
⅛ teaspoon salt
⅔ cup (130 g) granulated sugar
1 drop liquid food coloring (optional; I used blue)
3 tablespoons (30 g) rainbow nonpareil sprinkles

Sally Says

My favorite piping tip to use for making meringues is Ateco #849.

1. Preheat oven to 225°F (110°C). Line baking sheets with silicone baking mats. (I prefer silicone baking mats over parchment paper for this recipe because my meringues sometimes stick to parchment.) Set aside.

2. In a large bowl, using a handheld mixer or a stand mixer fitted with a whisk attachment, beat the egg whites, cream of tartar, and salt together on high speed until soft peaks form, about 3 minutes. Add the granulated sugar and continue beating on high speed until stiff peaks form, about 2 more minutes. Beat in the food coloring, if using, on low speed just until combined.

3. Using a tablespoon (No. 60 scoop) or a pastry bag fitted with a piping tip, spoon or pipe 1½-inch (4 cm) mounds, 2 inches (5 cm) apart, on the baking sheets. Sprinkle each lightly with nonpareil sprinkles.

4. Bake for 2 hours. Turn the oven off and let the meringues sit inside as the oven cools for 30 minutes.

5. Remove from the oven and allow the meringues to cool completely on the baking sheets. Once cool, use a flat spatula to help remove the meringues from the baking sheets.

6. Meringues will stay fresh in an airtight container at room temperature for up to 2 weeks.

MAKE-AHEAD TIP

Meringues stay fresh and taste wonderful for up to 2 weeks, so they're a great recipe to make a week or so before you need them. Baked meringues freeze well for up to 1 month. Since they are quite fragile, I recommend carefully arranging in a sturdy freezer-friendly container instead of a freezer bag.

Strawberries & Cream Cookie Cups

The dough for these "cups" is similar to that used for Sugar Cookie Sparkles (page 110), but I add an extra ounce (28 g) of cream cheese here (see *Sally Says* on page 124). What may be even better than the soft sugar cookie cup is the strawberry frosting on top. My secret for strawberry frosting is using freeze-dried strawberries. I always have trouble using real strawberries in frosting—they tend to curdle the butter! Instead, I grind the freeze-dried strawberries into a dust, add them to the frosting, and end up with a delicious, concentrated REAL strawberry flavor that doesn't compromise the frosting texture.

PREP TIME: 20 minutes   **TOTAL TIME:** 2 hours 20 minutes   **YIELD:** 46 to 48 cookies

Cookie Cups

3 cups (360 g) all-purpose flour
1½ teaspoons baking powder
½ teaspoon salt
1 cup (2 sticks, or 240 g) unsalted butter, softened to room temperature
3 ounces (85 g) block cream cheese, softened to room temperature
1 cup (100 g) granulated sugar
1 large egg, room temperature
2 teaspoons pure vanilla extract

Strawberry Frosting

½ cup (6 g) freeze-dried strawberries
½ cup (1 stick, or 240 g) unsalted butter, softened to room temperature
2 cups (240 g) confectioners' sugar
2 tablespoons (30 ml) heavy cream
1 teaspoon vanilla extract
pinch salt, if needed
¼ cup (40 g) rainbow sprinkles

1. Preheat oven to 350°F (180°C). Lightly grease two 24-count mini-muffin pans or spray with nonstick spray. Set aside.

2. **To make the cookie cups:** Whisk the flour, baking powder, and salt together in a medium bowl until combined. Set aside.

3. In a large bowl, using a handheld mixer or a stand mixer fitted with a paddle attachment, beat the butter and cream cheese together on medium-high speed until smooth, about 2 minutes. Add the granulated sugar and beat on medium-high speed until creamed, about 1 minute. Add the egg and vanilla extract, and beat on high speed until combined, about 1 minute. Scrape down the sides and up the bottom of the bowl and beat again as needed to combine.

4. Add the dry ingredients to the wet ingredients and mix on low speed until combined. The dough will be thick.

5. Roll balls of dough, 1 tablespoon of dough per cookie, and place each ball into its own cup in the muffin pans. Bake for 11 to 13 minutes, or until lightly browned on the sides.

6. Remove from the oven and allow to cool for 10 minutes in the pan, then transfer to a wire rack to cool completely before frosting.

7. **To make the frosting:** Using a food processor, process the freeze-dried strawberries into a powdery crumb. You should have around ¼ cup (6 g). Set aside.

8. In a large bowl, using a handheld mixer or stand mixer fitted with a whisk attachment, beat the butter on medium-high speed until creamy, about 1 minute. Add the confectioners' sugar, strawberry powder, cream, and vanilla extract. Beat on low speed for 30 seconds, then switch to high speed and beat for 2 minutes. Taste. Add a pinch of salt if the frosting is too sweet.

continued »

Sally Says

Why the extra ounce (28 g) of cream cheese in the dough? Well, we don't have to worry about the cookies overspreading from an extra wet ingredient because they have the walls of the muffin pan to hold them together. A little extra soft cream cheese is nothing but fabulous in these bite-size goodies!

9. Frost each cooled cookie cup as desired. I used a Wilton® #12 piping tip to decorate my cookies. Decorate with sprinkles.

10. Frosted cookie cups will stay fresh in an airtight container in the refrigerator for up to 1 week.

MAKE-AHEAD TIP

Prepare the cookie dough through step 4. Cover and chill the dough in the refrigerator for at least 1 hour and up to 4 days before continuing with step 5. Unfrosted cookie cups will stay fresh in an airtight container at room temperature for up to 3 days.

PIÑATA COOKIE SURPRISES

I'm slightly addicted to serving piñata-inspired treats. I have a piñata cake recipe on my blog, as well as piñata cupcakes. When cutting or biting into either, you experience a wave of sprinkles and tiny candies hiding inside. It was only a matter of time before a cookie version exploded into our lives! Making these cookies isn't all that tricky. Each cookie stack is composed of four cookies, with sweet royal icing acting as the "glue." The two middle cookies have secret holes in which the sprinkles are hidden. The best part is watching someone take that first bite!

PREP TIME: 1 hour 10 minutes   **TOTAL TIME:** 4 hours 10 minutes   **YIELD:** 96 cookies or 24 cookie stacks

4½ cups (540 g) all-purpose flour, plus more if needed for dough and for rolling out

1 teaspoon baking powder

½ teaspoon salt

1½ cups (3 sticks, or 360 g) unsalted butter, softened to room temperature

1½ cups (300 g) granulated sugar

2 large eggs, room temperature

1 tablespoon (15 ml) pure vanilla extract (yes, 1 full tablespoon!)

Traditional Royal Icing (page 15)

½ cup (80 g) sprinkles and/or tiny candies, plus more for topping

SALLY SAYS

If the cookie dough gets too soft and warm during step 7, place back in the refrigerator until cold to the touch.

1. Whisk the flour, baking powder, and salt together in a medium bowl. Set aside.

2. In a large bowl, using a handheld mixer or a stand mixer fitted with a paddle attachment, beat the butter on medium-high speed until smooth, about 1 minute. Add the granulated sugar and beat on medium-high speed until creamed, about 2 minutes. Add the eggs and vanilla extract, and beat on high speed until combined, about 1 minute. Scrape down the sides and up the bottom of the bowl and beat again as needed to combine.

3. Add the dry ingredients to the wet ingredients and mix on low speed until combined. If the dough seems too soft, you can add 1 tablespoon (8 g) more flour to make it a better consistency for rolling.

4. Divide the dough into 2 equal portions. Roll each portion out onto a piece of parchment paper or a lightly floured silicone baking mat (I prefer a nonstick silicone mat) to about ¼ inch (6 mm) thickness. The rolled-out dough can be any shape, as long as it is evenly ¼ inch (6 mm) thick.

5. Stack the 2 slabs of dough, with a piece of parchment paper between them, on a baking sheet and refrigerate for at least 1 hour (and up to 2 days). If chilling for more than 2 hours, cover the top slab of dough with a single piece of parchment paper.

6. Preheat oven to 350°F (180°C). Line baking sheets with parchment paper or silicone baking mats. Set aside.

7. Remove one of the slabs of dough slabs from the refrigerator and, using a 2-inch (5 cm) round cookie cutter, cut into circles. Reroll the remaining slab and continue cutting until all is used. Repeat with second slab of dough. You should have about 96 circles.

continued »

8. Using a 1-inch (2.5 cm) round cookie cutter, cut a hole in the center of 48 of the circles. Let's call these 48 cookies the "donut cookies" because of that center hole.

9. Place the whole circles and the donut cookies on separate baking sheets (because the donut cookies take 1 minute less to bake), placing all cookies 2 inches (5 cm) apart.

10. Bake the whole circles for about 10 minutes, or until lightly browned around the edges, and the donut cookies for about 9 minutes. Rotate the baking sheets halfway through the bake time.

11. Remove from the oven and allow the cookies to cool on the baking sheets for 5 minutes, then transfer to a wire rack to cool completely before assembling.

12. Using a piping bag fitted with a #5 piping tip, pipe a ring of Traditional Royal Icing around 1 whole cookie. Top with a donut cookie and press down to secure. Pipe a ring around the donut cookie and top with another donut cookie. Press down to secure. Fill the hole to the top with sprinkles (see photo, left). Pipe a ring around the uppermost donut cookie and top with a whole cookie. Decorate the top cookie with icing and garnish with sprinkles. Repeat with rest of cookies. Let the icing set for 2 hours.

13. Cookies will stay fresh in an airtight container at room temperature or in the refrigerator for up to 1 week.

MAKE-AHEAD TIP

I do not recommend freezing assembled piñata cookies. As described in step 5, you can chill the rolled-out cookie dough in the refrigerator for up to 2 days. You can also freeze the cookie dough (before rolling out in step 4) for up to 3 months; allow frozen dough to thaw overnight in the refrigerator and bring to room temperature before rolling out; then, in step 5, chill for only 30 minutes rather than 1 full hour.

Giant Funfetti Cookie Pizza

This recipe definitely puts the "fun" in funfetti. The dough comes together in a snap, and all you have to do is press it onto a pizza pan. Also, there's enough sprinkles to make a unicorn jealous.

PREP TIME: 25 minutes   **TOTAL TIME:** 2 hours   **YIELD:** 12 slices

Nonstick spray or butter, for greasing

1½ cups (180 g) all-purpose flour

1½ teaspoons cornstarch

1 teaspoon baking powder

½ teaspoon baking soda

¼ teaspoon salt

½ cup (1 stick, or 240 g) unsalted butter, softened to room temperature

¾ cup (150 g) granulated sugar

1 large egg, room temperature

1 teaspoon pure vanilla extract

⅔ cup (110 g) plus 2 tablespoons (20 g) sprinkles, divided

Vanilla Frosting (page 13)

3 or 4 drops red or pink liquid food coloring (optional)

Sally Says

You can also use the strawberry frosting from the Strawberries & Cream Cookie Cups (page 123) for this cookie pizza!

1. Preheat oven to 350°F (180°C). Grease a 12-inch (30 cm) pizza pan with nonstick spray or butter.

2. Whisk the flour, cornstarch, baking powder, baking soda, and salt together in a medium bowl. Set aside.

3. In a large bowl, using a handheld mixer or a stand mixer fitted with a paddle attachment, beat the butter on medium-high speed until smooth, about 1 minute. Add the granulated sugar and beat on medium-high speed until creamed, about 2 minutes. Add the egg and vanilla extract, and beat on high speed until combined, about 1 minute. Scrape down the sides and up the bottom of the bowl and beat again as needed to combine.

4. Add the dry ingredients to the wet ingredients and mix on low speed until combined. Beat in ⅔ cup (110 g) of the sprinkles.

5. Press the cookie dough onto the greased pizza pan, forming a large circle and leaving 1 inch (2.5 cm) of space from the edge (dough should be ½ inch, or 13 mm, thick). Place the pan into the refrigerator to chill for 30 minutes (or up to 1 day).

6. Bake the cookie pizza for 17 to 20 minutes, or until lightly browned on the edges. Remove from the oven and place the pan on a wire rack. Cool the cookie pizza completely before frosting.

7. If desired, add 3 drops of red food coloring to the Vanilla Frosting to create a pink shade. For a slightly darker pink, add 1 more drop. Frost cookie pizza as desired. I used a Wilton® #1M piping tip. Decorate with remaining 2 tablespoons (20 g) sprinkles.

8. Store frosted cookie pizza in the refrigerator in an airtight container for up to 1 week.

MAKE-AHEAD TIP

Prepare the cookie dough through step 4, cover tightly, and refrigerate for up to 1 day before continuing with step 5. Or you can prepare the recipe through step 5, cover the shaped cookie dough on the pizza pan, and refrigerate for up to 1 day before continuing with step 6. Unfrosted baked cookie pizza will stay fresh in an airtight container at room temperature for up to 3 days.

NUTS ABOUT NUTS

If you're anything like me, you cherish nuts in baked goods. My ten-year-old self would have read that sentence in disbelief, but as I've grown up and matured (a little), I've come to appreciate and downright ADORE nuts in cookies! Walnuts, pecans, peanuts, pistachios . . . the whole lot of them.

While this chapter focuses on nuts of all shapes, flavors, and sizes, one ingredient you'll find in most of the recipes is peanut butter. Now it's not in every single recipe over these next few pages, but it is the star in most.

In this chapter, you'll find an old standby: the classic peanut butter cookie. There are also fun variations swirled with Nutella®, thumbprints filled with caramel and jam, and flourless cookies, which happen to be my absolute favorite. For the best results, I suggest avoiding a natural or oily peanut butter; usually such a peanut butter yields dry, sandy cookies.

Things are about to get real nutty in 3, 2, 1 . . .

CRISSCROSS PEANUT BUTTER COOKIES

I couldn't write a cookie book without them! This is a new peanut butter cookie recipe I've been working on. You'll use shortening in addition to butter as the base of the dough. The reason for this is that I found that including too much butter diminishes the peanut butter flavor. Shortening gets the job done without depriving the peanut butter of its glory.

PREP TIME: 15 minutes   **TOTAL TIME:** 2 hours   **YIELD:** 48 cookies

2¼ cups (270 g) all-purpose flour
1 teaspoon baking powder
1 teaspoon baking soda
½ teaspoon salt
½ cup (1 stick, or 120 g) unsalted
    butter, softened to room temperature
½ cup (95 g) vegetable shortening,
    room temperature
1 cup (225 g) packed light brown sugar
1 cup (200 g) granulated sugar, divided
2 large eggs, room temperature
1¼ cups (325 g) creamy peanut butter
1 teaspoon pure vanilla extract

MAKE-AHEAD TIP

See page 12.

1. Whisk the flour, baking powder, baking soda, and salt together in a medium bowl. Set aside.

2. In a large bowl, using a handheld mixer or a stand mixer fitted with a paddle attachment, beat the butter and shortening together on medium-high speed until smooth, about 1 minute. Add the brown sugar and ½ cup (100 g) of the granulated sugar, and beat on medium-high speed until creamed, about 2 minutes. Add the eggs and beat on high speed until combined, about 1 minute. Scrape down the sides and up the bottom of the bowl and beat again as needed to combine. Add the peanut butter and vanilla extract, and beat on medium-high speed until combined.

3. Add the dry ingredients to the wet ingredients and mix on low speed until combined.

4. Cover and chill the dough in the refrigerator for at least 1 hour (and up to 4 days). If chilling for longer than 3 hours, allow it to sit at room temperature for at least 30 minutes before rolling and baking because the dough will be quite hard.

5. Preheat oven to 350°F (180°C). Line baking sheets with parchment paper or silicone baking mats. Set aside.

6. Roll balls of dough, 1 tablespoon of dough per cookie, then roll each in remaining ½ cup (100 g) granulated sugar to coat. Place the dough balls 3 inches (7.5 cm) apart on the baking sheets. Press a fork into the tops to create the crisscross pattern (see photo, left).

7. Bake for 12 to 13 minutes until lightly browned on the sides. The centers will look soft. Remove from the oven and allow the cookies to cool on the baking sheets for 5 minutes before transferring to a wire rack to cool completely.

8. Cookies will stay fresh in an airtight container at room temperature for up to 1 week.

Peanut Butter Nutella® Swirl Cookies

These decadent treats are the result of glorious peanut butter and sumptuous Nutella® joining forces. All you do here is swirl Nutella® into Crisscross Peanut Butter Cookies (page 132) and add a little extra flavor with peanut butter–flavored morsels. If you can't find peanut butter–flavored morsels at the store, use chocolate chips or chopped peanuts instead.

PREP TIME: 15 minutes　　**TOTAL TIME:** 2 hours　　**YIELD:** 52 cookies

2¼ cups (270 g) all-purpose flour

1 teaspoon baking powder

1 teaspoon baking soda

½ teaspoon salt

½ cup (1 stick, or 120 g) unsalted butter, softened to room temperature

½ cup (95 g) vegetable shortening, room temperature

1 cup (225 g) packed light brown sugar

1 cup (200 g) granulated sugar, divided

2 large eggs, room temperature

1¼ cups (325 g) creamy peanut butter

1 teaspoon pure vanilla extract

1½ cups (360 g) peanut butter–flavored morsels

6 tablespoons (115 g) Nutella®

MAKE-AHEAD TIP

See page 12.

1. Whisk the flour, baking powder, baking soda, and salt together in a medium bowl. Set aside.

2. In a large bowl, using a handheld mixer or a stand mixer fitted with a paddle attachment, beat the butter and shortening together on medium-high speed until smooth, about 1 minute. Add the brown sugar and ½ cup (100 g) of the granulated sugar, and beat on medium-high speed until creamed, about 2 minutes. Add the eggs and beat on high speed until combined, about 1 minute. Scrape down the sides and up the bottom of the bowl and beat again as needed to combine. Add the peanut butter and vanilla extract, and beat on medium-high speed until combined.

3. Add the dry ingredients to the wet ingredients and mix on low speed until combined. With the mixer running on low speed, beat in the peanut butter morsels. Once combined, beat in the Nutella® for 10 seconds. Don't completely mix it in; you want Nutella® swirls.

4. Cover and chill the dough in the refrigerator for at least 1 hour (and up to 4 days). If chilling for longer than 3 hours, allow it to sit at room temperature for at least 30 minutes before rolling and baking because the dough will be quite hard.

5. Preheat oven to 350°F (180°C). Line baking sheets with parchment paper or silicone baking mats. Set aside.

6. Roll balls of dough, 1 tablespoon of dough per cookie, then roll each in remaining ½ cup (100 g) granulated sugar to coat. Place the dough balls 3 inches (7.5 cm) apart on the baking sheets. Press a fork into the tops to create the crisscross pattern.

7. Bake for 12 to 13 minutes until lightly browned on the sides. The centers will look soft. Remove from the oven and allow the cookies to cool on the baking sheets for 5 minutes before transferring to a wire rack to cool completely.

8. Cookies will stay fresh in an airtight container at room temperature for up to 1 week.

Soft Peanut Butter Cookies

For those of you who take your peanut butter seriously, this recipe is for you. There are not only 2 whole cups (520 g) of peanut butter in the dough, but also 2 cups (376 g) of peanut butter candies. You only need to chill this soft peanut butter cookie dough for 1 hour, which means you'll have more than three dozen peanut butter cookies at your disposal in no time. Wait, is that a bad thing?

PREP TIME: 15 minutes   **TOTAL TIME:** 1 hour 45 minutes   **YIELD:** 42 cookies

2½ (300 g) cups all-purpose flour

1 teaspoon baking powder

1 teaspoon baking soda

½ teaspoon salt

1 cup (2 sticks, or 240 g) unsalted butter, softened to room temperature

1 cup (200 g) granulated sugar

¾ cup (170 g) packed light brown sugar

2 large eggs, room temperature

2 cups (520 g) creamy peanut butter

1½ teaspoons pure vanilla extract

2 cups (376 g) Reese's® Pieces®

MAKE-AHEAD TIP

See page 12.

1. Whisk the flour, baking powder, baking soda, and salt together in a medium bowl. Set aside.

2. In a large bowl, using a handheld mixer or a stand mixer fitted with a paddle attachment, beat the butter on medium-high speed until smooth, about 1 minute. Add the granulated sugar and brown sugar, and beat on medium-high speed until creamed, about 2 minutes. Add the eggs and beat on high speed until combined, about 1 minute. Scrape down the sides and up the bottom of the bowl and beat again as needed to combine. Add the peanut butter and vanilla extract, and beat on medium-high speed until combined.

3. Add the dry ingredients to the wet ingredients and mix on low speed until combined. Beat in the Reese's® Pieces. The dough will be thick and soft.

4. Cover and chill the dough in the refrigerator for at least 1 hour (and up to 4 days). If chilling for longer than 3 hours, allow it to sit at room temperature for at least 30 minutes before rolling and baking because the dough will be quite hard.

5. Preheat oven to 350°F (180°C). Line baking sheets with parchment paper or silicone baking mats. Set aside.

6. Roll balls of dough, about 2 heaping tablespoons of dough per cookie, and place 3 inches (7.5 cm) apart on the baking sheets. Bake for 13 to 14 minutes, until lightly browned on the sides. The centers will look very soft.

7. Remove from the oven. If the cookies are still very puffy, you can gently press down on the warm cookies with the back of a spoon. Allow the cookies to cool on the baking sheets for 5 minutes before transferring to a wire rack to cool completely.

8. Cookies will stay fresh in an airtight container at room temperature for up to 1 week.

Peanut Butter–Stuffed Cookie Cups

Do you know what peanut butter blossom cookies are? They're those delectable peanut butter cookies with a chocolate Hershey's Kiss® in the center, typically gracing holiday cookie trays. I have a recipe for them in my cookbook *Sally's Candy Addiction*. But let's discuss an alternative, shall we? This recipe uses the same cookie dough, but calls for baking it in a mini-muffin pan. And instead of a chocolate candy, we're going to press a Reese's® Peanut Butter Cup inside each. Warm and ready to eat in 30 minutes, this cookie is definitely a pleaser!

PREP TIME: 10 minutes   **TOTAL TIME:** 45 minutes   **YIELD:** 32 cookies

Nonstick spray or butter, for greasing
1¼ cups (150 g) all-purpose flour
½ teaspoon baking soda
¼ teaspoon salt
½ cup (1 stick, or 120 g) unsalted butter, softened to room temperature
½ cup (115 g) packed light brown sugar
¼ cup (50 g) granulated sugar
1 large egg, room temperature
¾ cup (195 g) creamy peanut butter
1 teaspoon pure vanilla extract
32 Reese's® Peanut Butter Cups Miniatures, unwrapped

MAKE AHEAD-TIP

See page 12.

 Sally Says
Because we're using a muffin pan, the cookies cannot spread, so we don't need to chill the dough.

1. Preheat oven to 350°F (180°C). Generously grease a 24-count mini-muffin pan with nonstick spray or butter. You will need to bake in 2 batches or use another 24-count mini-muffin pan since this recipe makes 32 cookies.

2. Whisk the flour, baking soda, and salt together in a medium bowl. Set aside.

3. In a large bowl, using a handheld mixer or a stand mixer fitted with a paddle attachment, beat the butter on medium-high speed until smooth, about 1 minute. Add the brown sugar and granulated sugar, and beat on medium-high speed until creamed, about 2 minutes. Add the egg and beat on high speed until combined, about 1 minute. Scrape down the sides and up the bottom of the bowl and beat again as needed to combine. Add the peanut butter and vanilla extract, and beat on medium-high speed until combined.

4. Add the dry ingredients to the wet ingredients and mix on low speed until combined. The dough will be thick and soft.

5. Roll balls of dough, 1 tablespoon of dough per cookie, and place each dough ball into its own pan cup. Bake for 10 minutes, or until lightly browned on the sides.

6. Remove from the oven and immediately press a peanut butter cup into each warm cookie cup. Allow to cool for 20 minutes before removing the cookies from the pan. Transfer cookie cups to a wire rack to cool completely before enjoying. (But they're also SO tasty when warm!)

7. Cookies will stay fresh in an airtight container at room temperature for up to 1 week.

Pecan Turtle Cookie Bars

Between the buttery shortbread crust, caramel-like pecan filling, and chocolate topping, it's hard to choose a favorite part of these three-layer cookie bars. If you like turtles—meaning, the candy—then you'll flip for these!

PREP TIME: 45 minutes   **TOTAL TIME:** 3 hours 45 minutes   **YIELD:** 24 bars

Crust
¾ cup (1½ sticks, or 180 g) unsalted butter, softened to room temperature
¾ cup (170 g) packed brown sugar
1¾ cups (210 g) all-purpose flour
¼ teaspoon pure vanilla extract
¼ teaspoon salt

Filling and Topping
14-ounce (397 g) can full-fat sweetened condensed milk
2 tablespoons (30 g) unsalted butter
1¾ cups (190 g) chopped pecans, divided
2 (4 ounces, or 113 g, each) bars milk or semi-sweet chocolate, coarsely chopped
coarse sea salt, for topping (optional)

MAKE-AHEAD TIP

The best way to make these bars in advance is to freeze them. Layer the cut baked bars between sheets of parchment paper and arrange them in a plastic container or freezer bag. Freeze for up to 3 months. Thaw overnight in the refrigerator and, if desired, bring to room temperature before serving.

1. Preheat oven to 350°F (180°C). Line a 9 × 13-inch (23 × 33 cm) baking pan with parchment paper, leaving enough overhang around the sides to easily lift out the contents. (I encourage using parchment for this recipe so that you can easily remove the confection as a whole and not cut into bars while in the pan.) Set aside.

2. **To make the crust:** In a large bowl, using a handheld mixer or a stand mixer fitted with a paddle attachment, beat the butter on medium-high speed until smooth, about 1 minute. Add the brown sugar and beat on medium-high speed until creamed, about 2 minutes. Add the flour, vanilla extract, and salt, and beat on medium speed until combined, about 1 minute. Scrape down the sides and up the bottom of the bowl and beat again as needed to combine. The dough will be soft and thick.

3. Press the dough evenly into the prepared baking pan. Bake for 15 minutes, or until the top and edges are lightly browned. Remove from the oven and allow to cool slightly as you prepare the filling. Do not turn off the oven.

4. **To make the filling:** Combine the sweetened condensed milk and butter in a medium heatproof bowl. Microwave for 1 minute, then stir to ensure the butter is completely melted. If not, microwave for 10 more seconds. Stir in 1½ cups (165 g) of the pecans. Pour evenly over the crust.

5. Bake for 16 to 17 minutes, until the filling is bubbling and light brown. Remove from the oven and allow to cool slightly.

6. Melt the chopped chocolate in a double boiler or in the microwave in 15-second increments, stopping and stirring after each until completely smooth. Pour on top of the bars and gently spread to coat the entire pan. Sprinkle with remaining ¼ cup (25 g) pecans and, if desired, sea salt.

7. Allow to cool in the pan. Once completely cooled, remove the confection from the pan by picking it up with the overhanging parchment paper. Cut into squares. Note: if shortbread is not completely cool, the bars will fall apart when cutting.

8. Bars will stay fresh in an airtight container at room temperature for up to 2 days or in the refrigerator for up to 1 week.

Flourless Peanut Butter Cookies

Not only are these peanut butter cookies completely flourless, they're also gluten free, dairy free, and made with only five simple ingredients. Peanut butter is the base ingredient and really all you'll taste. I use the crunchy variety for added texture, but creamy works, too! I prefer these cookies with coconut sugar, but you can use brown sugar instead. The recipe yields only 12 to 14 cookies and, trust me, you won't want to share a single one!

PREP TIME: 15 minutes   **TOTAL TIME:** 35 minutes   **YIELD:** 12 to 14 cookies

1 large egg, room temperature

1 cup (260 g) crunchy or creamy peanut butter

½ cup coconut sugar (72 g) or packed brown sugar (115 g)

1 teaspoon pure vanilla extract

1 teaspoon baking soda

MAKE-AHEAD TIP

See page 12.

Sally Says

As mentioned on page 9, I have the best luck using a commercial-brand peanut butter, such as Skippy® or Jif®, as opposed to a natural-style or oily peanut butter; the cookies come out very crumbly with a natural peanut butter.

1. Preheat oven to 350°F (180°C). Line baking sheets with parchment paper or silicone baking mats.

2. Whisk the egg in a large bowl until beaten. Using a rubber spatula or wooden spoon, stir in the peanut butter, sugar, vanilla extract, and baking soda until completely combined.

3. The dough will be a little greasy, but do your best to roll it into balls, using 1½ tablespoons of dough per cookie. Place 3 inches (7.5 cm) apart on the baking sheets.

4. Bake for 12 to 13 minutes, or until relatively set on the sides.

5. Remove from the oven and allow the cookies to cool on the baking sheets for 5 minutes before transferring to a wire rack to cool completely.

6. Cookies will stay fresh in an airtight container at room temperature for up to 1 week.

PISTACHIO PUDDING COOKIES WITH CHOCOLATE CHIPS

In this recipe for chocolate chip cookies, some of the flour and sugar are replaced with dry pudding mix. You can use any flavor pudding mix you want; pistachio happens to be my number one pick off the shelves. Remember to use only the dry mix in this cookie dough and not the add-ins that are required for making actual pudding!

PREP TIME: 15 minutes   **TOTAL TIME:** 1 hour 5 minutes   **YIELD:** 36 cookies

2¼ cups (270 g) all-purpose flour

1 teaspoon baking soda

½ teaspoon salt

1 cup (2 sticks, or 240 g) unsalted butter, softened to room temperature

½ cup (115 g) packed light brown sugar

½ cup (100 g) granulated sugar

3.4-ounce (96 g) box pistachio instant pudding mix

2 large eggs, room temperature

1 teaspoon pure vanilla extract

1½ cups (270 g) semi-sweet chocolate chips

¾ cup (95 g) chopped salted pistachio

MAKE-AHEAD TIP

See page 12.

1. Whisk the flour, baking soda, and salt together in a medium bowl. Set aside.

2. In a large bowl, using a handheld mixer or a stand mixer fitted with a paddle attachment, beat the butter on medium-high speed until smooth, about 1 minute. Add the brown sugar and granulated sugar, and beat on medium-high speed until creamed, about 2 minutes. Add the dry pudding mix, eggs, and vanilla extract, and beat on high speed until combined, about 2 minutes. Scrape down the sides and up the bottom of the bowl and beat again as needed to combine.

3. Add the dry ingredients to the wet ingredients and mix on low speed until combined. With the mixer running on low speed, add the chocolate chips and pistachios. The dough will be soft and thick. Cover and chill in the refrigerator for 20 minutes (and up to 4 days). If chilling for longer than 3 hours, allow it to sit at room temperature for at least 1 hour before rolling and baking because the dough will be quite hard and the cookies won't spread.

4. Preheat oven to 350°F (180°C). Line baking sheets with parchment paper or silicone baking mats. Set aside.

5. Roll balls of dough, about 1½ tablespoons of dough per cookie, and arrange 3 inches (7.5 cm) apart on the baking sheets.

6. Bake for 12 to 13 minutes, or until lightly browned on the sides. The centers will look very soft.

7. Remove from the oven and allow the cookies to cool on the baking sheets for 5 minutes before transferring to a wire rack to cool completely.

8. Cookies will stay fresh in an airtight container at room temperature for up to 1 week.

PB&J THUMBPRINTS

You can have cookies for breakfast (see my Banana Almond Berry Breakfast Cookies on page 52), so why not for lunch, too? These soft peanut butter cookies will make you feel like a kid again—just in case the previous chapter, with its abundance of sprinkles, doesn't do the job! These cookies are coated with crunchy, salty peanuts, which provide the perfect complement to the sweet jam-filled centers. Read through the recipe before you begin, and make sure you've allotted enough time. The cookie dough needs time to chill in the refrigerator, as do the dough balls after they're shaped.

PREP TIME: 25 minutes   **TOTAL TIME:** 4 hours   **YIELD:** 32 to 36 cookies

1¼ cups (150 g) all-purpose flour
½ teaspoon baking soda
¼ teaspoon salt
½ cup (1 stick, or 120 g) unsalted butter, softened to room temperature
½ cup (115 g) packed light brown sugar
¼ cup (50 g) granulated sugar
1 large egg, room temperature
¾ cup (195 g) creamy peanut butter
1 teaspoon pure vanilla extract
¾ cup (110 g) crushed salted peanuts
6 tablespoons (120 g) favorite jam or jelly

1. Whisk the flour, baking soda, and salt together in a medium bowl. Set aside.

2. In a large bowl, using a handheld mixer or a stand mixer fitted with a paddle attachment, beat the butter on medium-high speed until smooth, about 1 minute. Add the brown sugar and granulated sugar, and beat on medium-high speed until creamed, about 2 minutes. Add the egg and beat on high speed until combined, about 1 minute. Scrape down the sides and up the bottom of the bowl and beat again as needed to combine. Add the peanut butter and vanilla extract, and beat on medium-high speed until combined.

3. Add the dry ingredients to the wet ingredients and mix on low speed until combined. The dough will be thick and soft. Cover and chill the dough for at least 1 hour (and up to 2 days) in the refrigerator. If chilling for longer than 3 hours, allow it to sit at room temperature for 30 minutes before rolling because the dough will be quite hard.

4. Roll balls of dough, using 1 scant tablespoon of dough per cookie, then roll each ball into the crushed peanuts. Press your thumb or the handle tip of a rubber spatula or wooden spoon into the center of each dough ball to make an indentation. Place the dough balls on 1 or 2 large plates, cover loosely, and chill in the refrigerator for 2 hours (and up to 2 days). If chilling for longer than 3 hours, allow it to sit at room temperature for 30 minutes before baking because the dough will be quite hard and the cookies won't spread.

5. Preheat oven to 350°F (180°C). Line baking sheets with parchment paper or silicone baking mats.

6. Place the dough balls on the baking sheets 3 inches (7.5 cm) apart. Spoon ½ teaspoon of jam into each indentation.

7. Bake for 11 to 13 minutes, or until lightly browned on the sides. The jam won't look completely set, but it will set as the cookies cool.

continued »

8. Remove from the oven and allow the cookies to cool on the baking sheets for 5 minutes before transferring to a wire rack to cool completely.

9. Cookies will stay fresh in an airtight container at room temperature for 2 days or in the refrigerator for up to 1 week.

MAKE-AHEAD TIP

While you can make the dough ahead of time and chill in the refrigerator as described in steps 3 and 4, you can also freeze unbaked dough balls (sans peanut coating and indentations) for up to 3 months; if you opt for the latter, chill the dough balls for 1 hour—this ensures they are solid and will not stick together in the freezer. Allow frozen dough balls to thaw overnight in the refrigerator, then roll them in the peanuts and make an indentation in each with your thumb (as described in step 4), and continue on to step 5. Baked cookies, with their jam filling, freeze well for up to 3 months; thaw overnight in the refrigerator and, if desired, bring to room temperature before serving.

OUTRAGEOUS PEANUTTY CARAMEL THUMBPRINTS

Everything deserves a spoonful of homemade caramel, and that most definitely includes cookies! This cookie dough is flavored with peanut butter and cocoa, but the situation doesn't get outrageous until you roll the dough in crushed peanuts and top with caramel. Note that when making the caramel, it's a good idea to wear kitchen gloves to protect your hands from any hot splatter.

PREP TIME: 30 minutes   **TOTAL TIME:** 2 hours 15 minutes   **YIELD:** 36 cookies

Thumbprint Cookies

1½ cups (180 g) all-purpose flour

½ cup (43 g) unsweetened natural or Dutch-process cocoa powder

½ teaspoon baking soda

¼ teaspoon salt

½ cup (1 stick, or 120 g) unsalted butter, softened to room temperature

½ cup (115 g) packed light brown sugar

½ cup (50 g) granulated sugar

1 large egg, room temperature

¼ cup (65 g) creamy peanut butter

2 tablespoons (30 ml) milk

1 teaspoon pure vanilla extract

¾ cup (110 g) crushed salted peanuts

Homemade Caramel

1 cup (200 g) granulated sugar

6 tablespoons (¾ stick, or 180 g) unsalted butter, softened to room temperature, sliced into tablespoon pieces

½ cup (120 ml) heavy cream, room temperature

¼ teaspoon salt

1. **To make the cookies:** Whisk the flour, cocoa powder, baking soda, and salt together in a medium bowl. Set aside.

2. In a large bowl, using a handheld mixer or a stand mixer fitted with a paddle attachment, beat the butter on medium-high speed until smooth, about 1 minute. Add the brown sugar and granulated sugar, and beat on medium-high speed until creamed, about 2 minutes. Add the egg and beat on high speed until combined, about 1 minute. Scrape down the sides and up the bottom of the bowl and beat again as needed to combine. Add the peanut butter, milk, and vanilla extract, and beat on medium-high speed until combined.

3. Add the dry ingredients to the wet ingredients and mix on low speed until combined. The dough will be soft and thick. Cover and chill the dough in the refrigerator for at least 1 hour (and up to 4 days). If chilling for longer than 3 hours, allow it to sit at room temperature for 30 minutes before rolling and baking because the dough will be quite hard and the cookies won't spread.

4. Roll balls of dough, using 1 scant tablespoon of dough per cookie, then roll each ball into the crushed peanuts. Press your thumb or the handle tip of a rubber spatula or wooden spoon into the center of each dough ball to make an indentation. Place dough balls on 1 or 2 large plates, cover loosely, and chill in the refrigerator for a few minutes as the oven preheats.

5. Preheat oven to 350°F (180°C). Line baking sheets with parchment paper or silicone baking mats.

6. Place dough balls on the baking sheets 3 inches (7.5 cm) apart.

7. Bake for 12 to 13 minutes, or until relatively set on the sides.

8. Remove from the oven. If the indentations have puffed up, press the handle tip of a rubber spatula or wooden spoon into the cookies. Allow the cookies to cool on the baking sheets for 5 minutes, then transfer the cookies to a wire rack to cool completely before filling with caramel.

continued ❯❯

9. **To make the caramel:** Heat the sugar in a medium saucepan over medium heat, stirring constantly with a wooden spoon or heatproof rubber spatula. The sugar will form clumps and eventually melt into a thick brown liquid as you continue to stir. Once completely melted, immediately add the butter. The mixture will bubble rapidly. Continue to stir for 2 minutes. If the butter is not incorporating well, use a whisk and stir rapidly. Stir in the cream and allow to boil for 1 minute. Remove from heat and stir in the salt. Allow to cool for 10 minutes before adding to the thumbprints (see photo, left).

10. Spoon ½ to 1 teaspoon of the caramel into the indentation of each cookie, or however much is needed. Enjoy the cookies right away or wait until the caramel is relatively set, about 2 hours.

11. Cookies will stay fresh in an airtight container at room temperature for 2 days or in the refrigerator for up to 1 week.

MAKE-AHEAD TIP

You can make the cookie dough and chill it in the refrigerator for up to 4 days, as described in step 3, or you can freeze unbaked cookie dough balls (sans peanut coating and indents) for up to 3 months; If you opt for the latter, chill the dough balls for 1 hour—this ensures they are solid and will not stick together in the freezer. Allow frozen dough balls to thaw overnight in the refrigerator, then roll them in peanuts, make an indentation in each with your thumb, and continue on to step 5. Baked cookies, complete with caramel filling, freeze well for up to 3 months; thaw overnight in the refrigerator and, if desired, bring to room temperature before serving.

 ### SALLY SAYS

Have leftover caramel? A bowl of ice cream deserves a spoonful, too. You can cover and store any leftover caramel in the refrigerator for up to 2 to 3 weeks.

Serious Chocolate Cravings

This is the chapter where most of my random cookie creations landed. And, not surprisingly, they all include chocolate.

Over the next several decadent pages, you'll find a slew of calories. I mean cookie variations. My favorite brownie cookies make their debut, and there are stuffed cookies, a warm and gooey skillet cookie, ice cream cookiewiches, and many other sumptuous chocolate confections. Chocolate chips and cocoa powder appear in abundance—and I'm not shy about chocolate ganache, either. If you're confused about any of the ingredients used, flip to page 8 for some clarification.

I'm certain you'll love the last recipe in this chapter the most. It's a cookie before it becomes a cookie! Go ahead and grab a spoon now.

Chocolate Hazelnut Thumbprints

Let's kick the chapter off with a doubly-rich chocolate experience. The recipe for the cookie dough is the same as that for Rainbow Kiss Cookies (page 118). These cookies, though, will be rolled a little larger—and treated to a coating of chopped hazelnuts. As the cookies bake, the nuts develop a toasty flavor. The soft ganache, which provides these cookies with a deeply decadent center, is similar to the one used for Birthday Party Thumbprints (page 114), but is made with semi-sweet chocolate instead of white chocolate (and no food coloring comes into play).

PREP TIME: 35 minutes   **TOTAL TIME:** 1 hour 35 minutes   **YIELD:** 24 to 26 cookies

Thumbprint Cookies
1 cup (120 g) all-purpose flour
½ cup (43 g) unsweetened natural or
    Dutch-process cocoa powder
¼ teaspoon salt
½ cup (1 stick, or 240 g) unsalted
    butter, softened to room temperature
cup (130 g) granulated sugar
1 egg yolk, room temperature
2 tablespoons (30 ml) milk
1 teaspoon pure vanilla extract
¾ cup (85 g) finely chopped hazelnuts

Chocolate Ganache
3 ounces (85 g) semi-sweet chocolate,
    coarsely chopped
3 tablespoons (45 ml) heavy cream

1. Preheat oven to 350°F (180°C). Line baking sheets with parchment paper or silicone baking mats. Set aside.

2. **To make the cookies:** Whisk the flour, cocoa powder, and salt together in a medium bowl. Set aside.

3. In a large bowl, using a handheld mixer or a stand mixer fitted with a paddle attachment, beat the butter on medium-high speed until smooth, about 1 minute. Add the granulated sugar and beat on medium-high speed until creamed, about 2 minutes. Add the egg yolk, milk, and vanilla extract, and beat on high speed until combined, about 1 minute. Scrape down the sides and up the bottom of the bowl and beat again as needed to combine.

4. Add the dry ingredients to the wet ingredients and mix on low speed until combined.

5. Roll balls of dough, using 1 scant tablespoon of dough per cookie, then roll each ball into the hazelnuts to coat. Press your thumb or the handle tip of a rubber spatula or wooden spoon into the center of each dough ball to make an indentation. Place 3 inches (7.5 cm) apart on the baking sheets.

6. Bake the cookies for 11 to 12 minutes, until they appear set on the edges.

7. Remove from the oven. If the indentations have puffed up, press the handle tip of a rubber spatula or wooden spoon into the cookies. Allow the cookies to cool on the baking sheets for 5 minutes before transferring to a wire rack to cool completely.

continued »

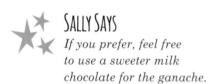

Sally Says

If you prefer, feel free to use a sweeter milk chocolate for the ganache.

8. **To make the ganache:** Place the chopped chocolate into a small heatproof bowl. Heat the cream in a small saucepan over medium heat, stirring occasionally. Once the cream begins to boil, immediately remove from the heat and pour over the chocolate. Stir gently and slowly until the ganache is smooth. Allow it to cool for 10 minutes before adding to the cookies. During this time, it will slowly thicken (see photo, left).

9. Once ganache is ready, spoon ½ to 1 teaspoon into the indentation of each completely cooled cookie, or however much is needed. Enjoy the cookies right away or wait until ganache is relatively set, about 2 hours.

10. Cookies will stay fresh in an airtight container at room temperature for 2 days or in the refrigerator for up to 1 week.

MAKE-AHEAD TIP

Prepare the cookie dough through step 4 and chill it in the refrigerator for up to 4 days; let it come to room temperature before continuing with step 5. Unbaked dough balls (sans nuts and indentations) freeze well for up to 3 months; if chilling for longer than 3 hours, allow them to sit at room temperature for 30 minutes before rolling and baking because the dough will be quite hard and the cookies won't spread. Allow them to thaw overnight in the refrigerator, then roll them in the hazelnuts, make an indentation into each with your thumb, and continue with step 6. Baked cookies, complete with ganache filling, freeze well for up to 3 months; thaw overnight in the refrigerator and, if desired, bring to room temperature before serving.

Striped Fudge Cookie Sandwiches

A fun homemade version of the delicious Keebler® brand cookie!

PREP TIME: 1 hour   **TOTAL TIME:** 2 hours 45 minutes   **YIELD:** 64 cookies or 32 sandwiches

Cookie Dough

2¼ (270 g) cups all-purpose flour, plus
   more if needed for the dough and for
   rolling out

½ teaspoon baking powder

¼ teaspoon salt

¾ cup (1½ sticks, 180 g) unsalted
   butter, softened to room temperature

¾ cup (150 g) granulated sugar

1 large egg, room temperature

2 teaspoons pure vanilla extract

Chocolate Ganache

3 ounces (85 g) semi-sweet chocolate,
   coarsely chopped

3 tablespoons (45 ml) heavy cream

Topping

2 ounces (56 g) semi-sweet chocolate,
   coarsely chopped

1. **Make the cookies:** Whisk the flour, baking powder, and salt together in a medium bowl. Set aside.

2. In a large bowl, using a handheld mixer or a stand mixer fitted with a paddle attachment, beat the butter on medium-high speed until smooth, about 1 minute. Add the granulated sugar and beat on medium-high speed until creamed, about 2 minutes. Add the egg and vanilla extract, and beat on high speed until combined, about 1 minute. Scrape down the sides and up the bottom of the bowl and beat again as needed to combine.

3. Add the dry ingredients to the wet ingredients and mix on low speed until combined. If the dough seems too soft, you can add 1 tablespoon (8 g) flour to make it a better consistency for rolling.

4. Divide the dough into 2 equal portions. Roll each portion out onto a piece of parchment paper or a lightly floured silicone baking mat (I prefer a nonstick silicone mat) to about ¼ inch (6 mm) thickness. The rolled-out dough can be any shape, as long as it is evenly ¼ inch (6 mm) thick.

5. Stack the 2 slabs of dough, with a piece of parchment paper between them, on a baking sheet and refrigerate for at least 1 hour (and up to 2 days). If chilling for more than 2 hours, cover the top slab of dough with a single piece of parchment paper.

6. Preheat oven to 350°F (180°C). Line baking sheets with parchment paper or silicone baking mats.

7. Remove one of the slabs of dough from the refrigerator and, using a 2-inch (5 cm) round cookie cutter, cut into circles. Reroll the remaining slab and continue cutting until all is used. Repeat with the second slab of dough. You should have about 64 circles.

8. Using a 1-inch (2.5 cm) round cookie cutter, cut a hole into the center of 32 of them. Let's call these 32 cookies the "donut cookies" because of that center hole.

continued »

9. Place the whole circles and the donut cookies on separate baking sheets (because the donut cookies take 1 minute less to bake), placing all cookies 2 inches (5 cm) apart. Bake the whole circles for about 10 minutes, or until lightly browned around the edges, and the donut cookies for about 9 minutes. Rotate the baking sheets halfway through bake time.

10. Remove from the oven. Allow the cookies to cool on the baking sheets for 5 minutes, then transfer to a wire rack to cool completely before assembling.

11. **To make the ganache:** Place the chopped chocolate into a small heatproof bowl. Heat the cream in a small saucepan over medium heat, stirring occasionally. Once the cream begins to boil, immediately remove from the heat and pour over the chocolate. Stir gently and slowly until the ganache is smooth. Allow it to cool for 10 minutes before adding to cookies. During this time, it will slowly thicken.

12. Once the ganache is ready, spread ½ teaspoon on each whole circle (see photo, left). Carefully top each with a donut cookie and press down gently to create a cookie sandwich.

13. **To make the topping:** Melt the chopped chocolate in a double boiler or in the microwave in 15-second increments, stopping and stirring after each until completely smooth. Drizzle over each sandwich. Allow the chocolate to set completely, about 30 minutes.

14. Cookies will stay fresh in an airtight container at room temperature for 2 days or in the refrigerator for up to 1 week.

MAKE-AHEAD TIP

You can chill the rolled-out cookie dough in the refrigerator for up to 2 days (see step 5), or you can freeze the cookie dough (before rolling out in step 4) for up to 3 months; if you opt for the latter, allow to thaw overnight in the refrigerator, then bring to room temperature before rolling out; chill for only 30 minutes in step 5 as opposed to 1 hour. Assembled cookie sandwiches freeze well for up to 3 months; allow cookies to thaw overnight in the refrigerator, then bring to room temperature before serving.

CHOCOLATE PRETZEL COOKIEWICHES

My friend Katy's favorite dessert on the planet is a cookie ice cream sandwich. In fact, she had a cookie ice cream sandwich bar at her wedding last year! While the ceremony was beautiful and the dancing was a blast, I think the biggest hit of the night were those cookie sandwiches. A cookie ice cream sandwich is such a simple idea and yet it's a massively underrated treat! Here we use a crisp chocolate chip cookie that will hold up against the soft ice cream. A roll in salty pretzels adds extra texture, but you could certainly use mini chocolate chips or nuts instead!

PREP TIME: 1 hour 30 minutes (includes the cookies)   **TOTAL TIME:** 3 hours   **YIELD:** 30 cookies or 15 cookie sandwiches

1 batch (30 cookies) Crispy-Edged Chocolate Chip Cookies (page 26), baked and cooled
2 quarts (2 L) chocolate ice cream
2 cups (90 g) pretzel pieces

1. Place 1 scoop of ice cream between 2 cookies. Press the 2 cookies together slightly to really sandwich the ice cream in. Roll the edges in pretzel pieces. Immediately wrap in plastic wrap and place in the freezer. Repeat with the remaining cookies, ice cream, and pretzels.

2. Freeze the sandwiches for at least 1 hour before enjoying.

3. Individually wrapped cookie sandwiches can be frozen for up to 2 weeks.

SALLY SAYS

My number one tip? Wrap each cookie sandwich immediately after you assemble it. My cookiewiches always start to melt unless I wrap them tightly and get them in the freezer FAST!

Midnight Brownie Cookies

Brownie cookies have been on my baking bucket list (you have one of those, too, right?) for about five years. I tested a few versions for this cookbook, and the recipe below came in first place with my friends and family. The cookies taste like fudge brownies, but they have these incredibly addictive crisp and chewy edges. I suggest using Dutch-process cocoa because it's slightly less acidic and will produce deeper, darker brownie cookies.

PREP TIME: 15 minutes   **TOTAL TIME:** 2 hours 45 minutes   **YIELD:** 20 to 22 cookies

4-ounce (113 g) bar semi-sweet chocolate, coarsely chopped

½ cup (120 ml) canola or vegetable oil

3 large eggs, room temperature

1 teaspoon pure vanilla extract

1¾ cups (210 g) all-purpose flour

1½ cups (300 g) granulated sugar

¼ cup (21 g) unsweetened Dutch-process cocoa powder

1½ teaspoons baking powder

1 teaspoon salt

MAKE-AHEAD TIP

See page 12.

Sally Says

These brownie cookies are incredible on their own, but for an even more decadent treat, drizzle the cooled cookies with Homemade Caramel, used in Outrageous Peanutty Caramel Thumbprints (page 149).

1. In a large heatproof bowl, melt the chopped chocolate in the microwave in 15-second increments, stopping and stirring after each until completely smooth. Allow to cool down for 5 minutes. Whisk in the oil, eggs, and vanilla extract.

2. Whisk the flour, granulated sugar, cocoa powder, baking powder, and salt together in a separate, medium bowl.

3. Add the dry ingredients to the wet ingredients and, using a handheld mixer or stand mixer fitted with a whisk attachment, beat together until combined. The dough will be very thick and a little greasy.

4. Cover and chill the dough in the refrigerator for at least 2 hours (and up to 4 days). If chilling for longer than 3 hours, allow it to sit at room temperature for at least 30 minutes before rolling and baking because the dough will be quite hard.

5. Preheat oven to 350°F (180°C). Line baking sheets with parchment paper or silicone baking mats. Set aside.

6. Roll balls of dough, about 1½ tablespoons of dough per cookie, and place 3 inches (7.5 cm) apart on the baking sheets.

7. Bake for 13 to 14 minutes, or until the tops begin cracking.

8. Remove from the oven and allow the cookies to cool on the baking sheets for 5 minutes before transferring to a wire rack to cool completely.

9. Cookies will stay fresh in an airtight container at room temperature for up to 1 week.

Brown Butter Toffee Chocolate Chip Cookies

After several (seriously, several!!) attempts, I landed on this recipe for salty-sweet, brown butter chocolate chip cookies with crisp edges and soft chewy centers. The key is to brown only half of the butter, giving the cookies that distinct brown butter flavor and chewy centers. Creaming the other half of the butter creates the softer centers. Ladies and gentlemen, we've reached our cookie destination.

PREP TIME: 30 minutes   **TOTAL TIME:** 4 hours   **YIELD:** 40 cookies

1 cup (2 sticks, or 240 g) unsalted butter, softened to room temperature, divided

2½ cups (300 g) all-purpose flour

1 teaspoon baking soda

1 teaspoon baking powder

½ teaspoon salt

1 cup (225 g) packed brown sugar

½ cup (100 g) granulated sugar

2 large eggs, room temperature

2 teaspoons pure vanilla extract

1 cup (180 g) semi-sweet chocolate chips

1 cup (240 g) toffee bits (such as Heath Bits 'o Brickle Toffee Bits)

MAKE AHEAD-TIP

See page 12.

1. Brown the butter: Have a large heatproof bowl handy. Cut ½ cup (1 stick, or 120 g) of the butter into slices. Place sliced butter in a light-colored skillet over medium heat. (The light color will help you determine when the butter starts to brown.) Whisking constantly, melt the butter. The butter will begin to foam. After 5 to 8 minutes, it will begin browning—you'll notice lightly browned specks beginning to form at the bottom of the pan (see photo, page 18) and there will be a nutty aroma. Once browned, immediately remove from the heat to stop the browning process and pour into the heatproof bowl. Allow the butter to cool in the refrigerator for 10 minutes.

2. Whisk the flour, baking soda, baking powder, and salt together in a medium bowl. Set aside.

3. In a large bowl, using a handheld mixer or a stand mixer fitted with a paddle attachment, beat the remaining ½ cup (1 stick, or 120 g) butter on medium-high speed until smooth, about 1 minute. Add the brown sugar and granulated sugar, and beat on medium-high speed until creamed, about 2 minutes. Add the browned butter, eggs, and vanilla extract, and beat on high speed until combined, about 1 minute. Scrape down the sides and up the bottom of the bowl and beat again as needed to combine.

4. Add the dry ingredients to the wet ingredients and mix on low speed until combined. Beat in the chocolate chips and toffee bits. The dough will be soft.

5. Cover and chill the dough in the refrigerator for at least 3 hours (and up to 4 days). If chilling for longer than 3 hours, allow it to sit at room temperature for at least 30 minutes before rolling and baking because the dough will be quite hard.

6. Preheat oven to 350°F (180°C). Line baking sheets with parchment paper or silicone baking mats. Set aside.

7. Roll balls of dough, about 1½ tablespoons of dough per cookie, and place 3 inches (7.5 cm) apart on the baking sheets. Bake for 12 to 14 minutes, until lightly browned on the sides. The centers will look soft.

8. Remove from the oven and allow the cookies to cool on the baking sheets for 5 minutes before transferring to a wire rack to cool completely. Cookies will stay fresh in an airtight container at room temperature for up to 1 week.

WARM CHOCOLATE CHUNK SKILLET COOKIE

If soft and gooey chocolate chip cookies are your favorite, this skillet cookie has your name written all over it. It's perfect for a gathering with friends where you can all sit around the table and eat the warm cookie right out of the pan. Top with ice cream to make it sundae-style. The best part is that you don't have to chill the dough before baking. This is a quick and majorly indulgent treat!

PREP TIME: 10 minutes   **TOTAL TIME:** 40 minutes   **YIELD:** serves 8 to 10

2¼ cups (270 g) all-purpose flour

1 teaspoon cornstarch

1 teaspoon baking soda

½ teaspoon salt

¾ cup (1½ sticks, or 180 g) unsalted butter, softened to room temperature

1 cup (225 g) packed brown sugar

¼ cup (50 g) granulated sugar

1 large egg plus 1 egg yolk, both at room temperature

2 teaspoons pure vanilla extract

1½ cups (270 g) semi-sweet chocolate chunks or chips

coarse sea salt, for topping

ice cream, for serving (optional)

chocolate syrup, for serving (optional)

1. Preheat oven to 350°F (180°C). Lightly grease a 10-inch (25 cm) oven-safe skillet.

2. Whisk the flour, cornstarch, baking soda, and salt together in a medium bowl. Set aside.

3. In a large bowl, using a handheld mixer or a stand mixer fitted with a paddle attachment, beat the butter on medium-high speed until smooth, about 1 minute. Add the brown sugar and granulated sugar, and beat on medium-high speed until creamed, about 2 minutes. Add the egg, egg yolk, and vanilla extract, and beat on high speed until combined, about 1 minute. Scrape down the sides and up the bottom of the bowl and beat again as needed to combine.

4. Add the dry ingredients to the wet ingredients and mix on low speed until combined. Beat in the chocolate chunks. The dough will be soft.

5. Press the dough into the prepared skillet. Sprinkle with sea salt.

6. Bake for 23 to 25 minutes, or until the edges are lightly browned and set. You want the middle to be slightly underbaked.

7. Remove from the oven and allow to cool for 5 minutes before serving. Top with ice cream and chocolate sauce, if desired, and either serve individual pieces or just give everyone a spoon and let them eat right out of the pan!

8. Cover leftovers, without ice cream, tightly and store in the refrigerator for up to 4 days.

MAKE-AHEAD TIP

You can make the cookie dough through step 4 and chill it in an airtight container in the refrigerator for up to 4 days. Before using, allow to come to room temperature, then continue with step 5. You can also freeze the cookie dough for up to 3 months; thaw overnight in the refrigerator and bring to room temperature before continuing with step 5.

Dark Chocolate Peanut Butter–Stuffed Cookies

Yep, these cookies are love at first bite. Three pieces of advice: (1) Have a paper towel nearby when you're assembling the cookies, as this is a sticky cookie dough—the result of all that cocoa powder and butter; (2) chilling the cookie dough is massively important; and (3) a tall glass of cold milk is required.

PREP TIME: 30 minutes   **TOTAL TIME:** 3 hours   **YIELD:** 16 large cookies

1 cup (120 g) all-purpose flour
⅔ cup (57 g) unsweetened natural cocoa powder
1 teaspoon baking soda
⅛ teaspoon salt
½ cup (1 stick, or 120 g) unsalted butter, softened to room temperature
½ cup (115 g) packed brown sugar
½ cup (100 g) granulated sugar
1 large egg, room temperature
1 teaspoon pure vanilla extract
2 tablespoons (30 ml) milk
16 Reese's® Peanut Butter Cups Miniatures, unwrapped

MAKE AHEAD-TIP

See page 12.

Sally Says

It goes without saying that these cookies taste phenomenal after cooling for just a few minutes, so feel free to enjoy them then. The peanut butter cup will be all melty, and the cookies will be ultrasoft. YUM.

1. Whisk the flour, cocoa powder, baking soda, and salt together in a medium bowl. Set aside.

2. In a large bowl, using a handheld mixer or a stand mixer fitted with a paddle attachment, beat the butter on medium-high speed until smooth, about 1 minute. Add the brown sugar and granulated sugar, and beat on medium-high speed until creamed, about 2 minutes. Add the egg and vanilla extract, and beat on high speed until combined, about 1 minute. Scrape down the sides and up the bottom of the bowl and beat again as needed to combine.

3. Add the dry ingredients to the wet ingredients and mix on low speed until combined. Finally, beat in the milk. The dough will be soft and sticky.

4. Cover and chill the dough in the refrigerator for at least 2 hours (and up to 4 days). If chilling for longer than 3 hours, allow it to sit at room temperature for at least 30 minutes before rolling and baking because the dough will be quite hard.

5. Preheat oven to 350°F (180°C). Line baking sheets with parchment paper or silicone baking mats. Set aside.

6. Roll balls of dough, using about 1 tablespoon of dough for each cookie. Make a thumbprint in one of the dough balls, press a miniature peanut butter cup candy into the center, and top with another dough ball. Mold the dough around the edges of the peanut butter cup candy and roll it between your hands to ensure the candy is completely hidden inside. Repeat with remaining dough. Place the dough balls 3 inches (7.5 cm) apart on the cookie sheets.

7. Bake for 12 to 13 minutes, or until the cookies begin to crack slightly at the top. Remove from the oven and allow the cookies to cool on the baking sheets for 5 minutes before transferring to a wire rack to cool completely.

8. Cookies will stay fresh in an airtight container at room temperature for up to 1 week.

Double Chocolate Coconut Macaroons

I can't let you step away from this book without trying these completely divine cookies. The recipe combines chocolate and its BFF—for once, I'm not referring to peanut butter—coconut. The best part is that these coconut macaroons couldn't be easier. Like my Cherry Almond Coconut Macaroons (page 70), you'll need a food processor to really grind up the coconut in step 3. The cookies are bound together and stay moist inside with egg whites and, you guessed it, chocolate. They're also inherently gluten free.

PREP TIME: 20 minutes   **TOTAL TIME:** 1 hour   **YIELD:** 20 to 24 cookies

6 ounces (170 g) semi-sweet chocolate, coarsely chopped, divided
14-ounce (396 g) bag sweetened shredded coconut (about 5⅓ cups)
½ cup (100 g) granulated sugar
⅓ cup (28 g) unsweetened natural or Dutch-process cocoa powder
¼ teaspoon salt
3 large egg whites

MAKE-AHEAD TIP

Prepare the macaroon mixture through step 3, then transfer to a bowl, cover tightly, and refrigerate for up to 4 days before continuing with step 4. Baked macaroons, without the chocolate coating, freeze well for up to 3 months; thaw overnight in the refrigerator before dunking into the chocolate and serving.

1. Preheat oven to 350°F (180°C). Line baking sheets with parchment paper or silicone baking mats. Set aside.

2. Melt 2 ounces (56 g) of the chopped chocolate in a double boiler or in the microwave in 15-second increments, stopping and stirring after each until completely smooth. Set aside.

3. In a large food processor, pulse the coconut until very finely chopped. Add the granulated sugar, cocoa powder, and salt, and pulse until relatively combined. Add the egg whites and the melted chocolate, and pulse until the entire mixture comes together.

4. Scoop balls of the mixture, about 1½ tablespoons (No. 40 scoop) per cookie, and place 2 inches (5 cm) apart on the baking sheets. The macaroons won't spread too much.

5. Bake for 15 to 18 minutes, or until set.

6. Remove from the oven and allow the macaroons to cool on the baking sheets for 15 minutes before transferring to a wire rack to cool completely.

7. Melt the remaining 4 ounces (113 g) chocolate in the same manner as in step 2. Dunk the bottom of each cooled macaroon into the chocolate. Allow the chocolate to set at room temperature or in the refrigerator for 30 minutes before enjoying.

8. Macaroons will stay fresh in an airtight container in the refrigerator for up to 1 week.

Hot Cocoa Cookies

Cozy cup of hot cocoa, you've met your match! The trick to these cookies is to slightly underbake them, stick a few marshmallows into the top of each, and then place the cookies back in the oven so the marshmallows melt slightly. To secure the marshmallows on top of the cookies, drizzle with milk chocolate. Every chilly day needs a batch!

PREP TIME: 15 minutes   **TOTAL TIME:** 1 hour   **YIELD:** 32 to 34 cookies

2¾ cups (330 g) all-purpose flour

⅔ cup (80 g) dry hot cocoa mix (about 4 standard packets)

1 teaspoon baking soda

1 teaspoon salt

1 cup (2 sticks, or 240 g) unsalted butter, softened to room temperature

1 cup (200 g) granulated sugar

½ cup (100 g) packed brown sugar

2 large eggs, room temperature

1½ teaspoons pure vanilla extract

1¼ cups (225 g) mini or regular-size chocolate chips

¾ cup (40 g) miniature marshmallows

4-ounce (113 g) bar milk chocolate, coarsely chopped

MAKE AHEAD-TIP

See page 12.

Sally Says

Remember to use the dry hot cocoa mix right out of the package. Do not prepare the hot cocoa and pour the liquid into the cookie dough. That would be a mess!

1. Preheat oven to 350°F (180°C). Line baking sheets with parchment paper or silicone baking mats. Set aside.

2. Whisk the flour, hot cocoa mix, baking soda, and salt together in a medium bowl. Set aside.

3. In a large bowl, using a handheld mixer or a stand mixer fitted with a paddle attachment, beat the butter on medium-high speed until smooth, about 1 minute. Add the granulated sugar and brown sugar, and beat on medium-high speed until creamed, about 2 minutes. Add the eggs and vanilla extract, and beat on high speed until combined, about 1 minute. Scrape down the sides and up the bottom of the bowl and beat again as needed to combine.

4. Add the dry ingredients to the wet ingredients and mix on low speed until combined. With the mixer running on low speed, add the chocolate chips. The dough will be soft and thick.

5. Roll balls of dough, about 1½ tablespoons of dough per cookie, and place 3 inches (7.5 cm) apart on the baking sheets.

6. Bake for 10 to 11 minutes. Remove from the oven and gently stick 4 or 5 marshmallows into the top of each cookie. Place back in the oven and bake for 2 more minutes to slightly melt the marshmallows.

7. Remove from the oven and allow to cool on the baking sheets for 5 minutes.

8. Meanwhile, melt the chopped chocolate in a double boiler or in the microwave in 15-second increments, stopping and stirring after each until completely smooth. Drizzle over the warm cookies. Allow the chocolate to set completely, about 20 minutes, before enjoying.

9. Cookies will stay fresh in an airtight container at room temperature for up to 4 days or in the refrigerator for up to 1 week.

Chocolate Chip Cookie Dough Dip

Baked cookies are, of course, delicious, but what about the stage right before? I'm talking chocolate chip cookie dough—that tempting bowl of dreamy, creamy goodness we all know tastes even better than its baked destiny. Here we'll ditch the raw eggs and flour and replace them with safe-to-consume milk and oat flour. This recipe includes instructions for making the oat flour yourself with a food processor, but you can certainly buy oat flour (if you go with the latter option, replace the 2 cups (180 g) of oats with 1½ cups (180 g) of oat flour). I serve this dessert dip with graham crackers, apple slices, pretzels, and vanilla wafer cookies, but who am I kidding? It's clearly best eaten with a spoon.

PREP TIME: 10 minutes   **TOTAL TIME:** 10 minutes   **YIELD:** 2½ cups

2 cups (180 g) old-fashioned whole rolled oats
½ cup (1 stick, or 120 g) unsalted butter, softened to room temperature
⅔ cup (150 g) packed brown sugar
¼ cup (50 g) granulated sugar
1 teaspoon pure vanilla extract
½ teaspoon salt
1 to 2 tablespoons (15 to 30 ml) milk
¾ cup (135 g) mini or 1 cup (180 g) regular-size semi-sweet chocolate chips

1. In a large food processor, pulse the oats until finely ground into a powder consistency (see photo, left). You do not want any large chunks of oats. You should end up with about 1½ cups (180 g) of oat flour, give or take. Set aside.

2. In a large bowl, using a handheld mixer or a stand mixer fitted with a paddle attachment, beat the butter on medium-high speed until smooth, about 1 minute. Add the brown sugar and granulated sugar, and beat on medium-high speed until creamed, about 2 minutes. Add the vanilla extract and beat on high speed until combined, about 1 minute. Add the oat flour, salt, and 1 tablespoon (15 ml) of milk. Beat on medium-high speed until combined. If the dough is a little too thick, add another tablespoon (15 ml) of milk. Beat in the chocolate chips until combined.

3. Spoon the cookie dough into a serving bowl.

4. Dip stays fresh in an airtight container in the refrigerator for up to 5 days.

MAKE AHEAD-TIP

While you can prepare the cookie dough dip up to 5 days in advance, and simply cover and store it in the refrigerator until you're ready to enjoy, you can also freeze it for up to 3 months; if you opt for the latter, thaw overnight in the refrigerator before serving.

Sally Says
Thanks to the oats, this cookie dough dip lends itself well to an oatmeal raisin twist. Simply add a dash of cinnamon and replace the chocolate chips with 1 heaping cup (145 g) of raisins. Then wave goodbye to your self-control.

FIND YOUR FLAVOR

Pumpkin and lemon and maple, oh my! If you haven't found the sweet flavor you adore most in this cookbook, I promise this chapter will have exactly what you're craving.

Not only will you find a large variety of cookie flavors—including butterscotch and cinnamon apple—over the next several pages, but you'll discover many different types of cookies as well. From drop cookies and no-bakes to sandwich cookies and cookie cups, this collection of recipes reminds us that cookies come in many shapes, sizes, and flavors. What a way to close out the book! There's a cookie for everyone to love.

SPICED PUMPKIN WHOOPIE PIES

Whoopie! The super-moist, spiced cookies used for these whoopie pies start out with cookie dough that is quite similar in texture to cake batter. While the cakey cookies are wonderful on their own, they're not complete until you add a generous layer of cream cheese frosting between them.

PREP TIME: 20 minutes   **TOTAL TIME:** 1 hour 45 minutes   **YIELD:** 24 cookies or 12 whoopie pies

Cookies

1½ cups (180 g) all-purpose flour
½ teaspoon baking powder
½ teaspoon baking soda
½ teaspoon salt
1½ teaspoons ground cinnamon
½ teaspoon ground cloves
½ teaspoon ground ginger
½ teaspoon ground nutmeg
½ cup (120 ml) vegetable oil
15-ounce (425 g) can pumpkin purée
   (not pumpkin pie filling)
1 large egg, room temperature
¾ cup (170 g) packed brown sugar
¼ cup (50 g) granulated sugar
1½ teaspoons pure vanilla extract

Cream Cheese Frosting

6 ounces (170 g) block cream cheese,
   softened to room temperature
¼ cup (½ stick, or 60 g) unsalted
   butter, softened to room temperature
1½ cups (180 g) confectioners' sugar
½ teaspoon pure vanilla extract

1. Preheat oven to 350°F (180°C). Line baking sheets with parchment paper or silicone baking mats. Set aside.

2. **To make the cookies:** Whisk the flour, baking powder, baking soda, salt, cinnamon, cloves, ginger, and nutmeg together in a large bowl and set aside.

3. In a medium bowl, whisk the oil, pumpkin purée, egg, brown sugar, granulated sugar, and vanilla extract together. Pour the wet ingredients into the dry ingredients and whisk until completely combined. The dough will be sticky.

4. Spoon mounds of batter, about 1½ tablespoons per cookie, onto the prepared baking sheets about 3 inches (7.5 cm) apart. Bake the cookies for 11 to 13 minutes, or until the centers appear set.

5. Remove from the oven and allow to cool on the baking sheets for 5 minutes before transferring to a wire rack to cool completely, about 1 hour.

6. **To make the frosting:** In a medium bowl, using a handheld mixer or a stand mixer fitted with a whisk attachment, beat the cream cheese and butter together on medium-high speed until completely smooth. Add the confectioners' sugar and vanilla extract, and beat on low speed for 20 seconds, then increase to high speed until combined, about 1 minute.

7. Pair the cookies up based on their similar shapes and sizes. Spread cream cheese frosting onto the flat side of one cookie and sandwich with the other. Repeat with remaining cookies and frosting.

8. Cover leftover whoopie pies and store in the refrigerator for up to 1 week.

MAKE AHEAD-TIP

Baked whoopie pies, wrapped individually, freeze well for up to 3 months; allow to thaw overnight in the refrigerator and, if desired, bring to room temperature before serving.

Pumpkin Spice Sugar Cookies

How adorable are these pumpkin cookies?! This is my basic sugar cookie dough (see Cookie Cutter Sugar Cookies on page 32), with pumpkin pie spice and cinnamon added. These cookies, with their spot-on fall flavor and soft centers, were gobbled up at a Halloween party last year. Decorating them with Traditional Royal Icing (page 15) isn't too tricky, but you can use my easier alternative, Glaze Icing (page 14).

PREP TIME: 1 hour   **TOTAL TIME:** 4 hours   **YIELD:** 28 (3-inch, or 7.5 cm) cookies or 60 (2-inch, or 5 cm) cookies

2¼ cups (270 g) all-purpose flour, plus more for the dough if needed and for rolling out

1½ teaspoons pumpkin pie spice

½ teaspoon ground cinnamon

½ teaspoon baking powder

¼ teaspoon salt

¾ cup (1½ sticks, or 180 g) unsalted butter, softened to room temperature

¾ cup (150 g) granulated sugar

1 large egg, room temperature

2 teaspoons pure vanilla extract

Traditional Royal Icing (page 15) or Glaze Icing (page 14)

1. Whisk the flour, pumpkin pie spice, cinnamon, baking powder, and salt together in a medium bowl. Set aside.

2. Continue with step 2 in Cookie Cutter Sugar Cookies (page 32).

MAKE AHEAD-TIP

As mentioned in the recipe instructions, you can chill the rolled-out cookie dough in the refrigerator for up to 2 days (see step 5), but you can also freeze the cookie dough (before rolling out in step 4) for up to 3 months. If you opt for the latter, allow the dough to thaw overnight in the refrigerator, then bring to room temperature before rolling out; in this situation, when you get to step 5, chill the dough for only 30 minutes as opposed to 1 hour. Undecorated cookies freeze well for up to 3 months; before icing or serving, thaw overnight in the refrigerator. I do not recommend freezing with icing on top.

 ### Sally Says

To create the pumpkin shapes in this photo, I used 2 different sizes of pumpkin-shaped cookie cutters: a 3-inch (7.5 cm) one and a 2-inch (5 cm) one. I used Traditional Royal Icing on the pictured cookies, with Wilton® #5 Round Decorating Tip for decorating. To create texture and lines on the pumpkins, pipe the outer 2 sections and the middle section. Wait until that icing is relatively dry, then pipe the remaining 2 sections as well as the stem.

BUTTERSCOTCH NO-BAKES

I remember eating these around the holidays when I was little. I've always loved butterscotch and peanut butter together, but hadn't really revisited my mom's recipe as an adult. I'm kicking myself for waiting twenty years to make these crunchy, crispy, undoubtedly rich treats—not only because they're lip-smacking delish, but also because they're so darn easy, with just three ingredients!

PREP TIME: 15 minutes   **TOTAL TIME:** 45 minutes   **YIELD:** 30 cookies

11-ounce (311 g) bag butterscotch
   morsels
¾ cup (195 g) creamy peanut butter
4 cups (120 g) cornflakes cereal

MAKE AHEAD-TIP

These butterscotch cookies can be frozen for up to 3 months after you refrigerate them in step 4; thaw overnight in the refrigerator before enjoying.

1. Line a baking sheet with parchment paper or silicone baking mat. Make sure there is enough room in your refrigerator for the baking sheet.

2. Combine the butterscotch morsels and peanut butter together in a medium saucepan over medium heat. Constantly whisk until completely melted and combined. Remove from the heat and stir in the cornflakes until combined.

3. Using a tablespoon (No. 60 scoop), drop mounds of the mixture on the lined baking sheet 2 inches (5 cm) apart.

4. Refrigerate the cookies, right on the baking sheet, uncovered, for at least 30 minutes before enjoying.

5. Cookies will stay fresh in an airtight container in the refrigerator for up to 1 week.

Glazed Soft Maple Cookies

In other words, pancake cookies. These super-soft gems will melt in your mouth and remind you that cookies are completely appropriate at the breakfast table. Don't be discouraged when you're mixing up the cookie dough. It's a very soft dough—almost like a thick cake batter.

PREP TIME: 25 minutes   **TOTAL TIME:** 2 hours   **YIELD:** 24 cookies

Cookies
2½ cups (300 g) all-purpose flour
½ teaspoon baking soda
1 teaspoon salt
½ cup (1 stick, or 120 g) unsalted butter, softened to room temperature
1¼ cups (285 g) packed brown sugar
½ cup (160 g) pure maple syrup (use the real stuff!)
2 large eggs, room temperature
½ cup (115 g) sour cream, room temperature
1 teaspoon pure vanilla extract

Maple Glaze
¼ cup (½ stick, or 60 g) unsalted butter
½ cup (160 g) pure maple syrup
1½ cups (180 g) sifted confectioners' sugar
⅛ teaspoon salt

1. Preheat oven to 350°F (180°C). Line baking sheets with parchment paper or silicone baking mats. Set aside.

2. **To make the cookies:** Whisk the flour, baking soda, and salt together in a medium bowl. Set aside.

3. In a large bowl, using a handheld mixer or a stand mixer fitted with a paddle attachment, beat the butter on medium-high speed until smooth, about 1 minute. Add the brown sugar and beat on medium-high speed until creamed, about 2 minutes. Add the maple syrup, eggs, sour cream, and vanilla extract, and beat on high speed until combined, about 2 minutes. Scrape down the sides and up the bottom of the bowl and beat again as needed to combine.

4. Add the dry ingredients to the wet ingredients and mix on low speed until combined. The dough will be very soft.

5. Scoop balls of dough, about 1½ tablespoons (No. 40 scoop) of dough per cookie, and place 3 inches (7.5 cm) apart on the baking sheets. Bake for 13 to 14 minutes, or until the tops spring back when lightly touched and the edges are lightly browned.

6. Remove from the oven and allow to cool on the baking sheets for 5 minutes before transferring to a wire rack to cool completely.

7. **To make the glaze:** Whisk the butter and maple syrup together in a small saucepan over medium heat until the butter is completely melted and is combined with the syrup. Remove from the heat and whisk in the confectioners' sugar and salt. Set aside to cool for 20 minutes.

8. Spoon glaze on top of each cooled cookie. Allow glaze to set completely, 30 minutes, before serving.

9. Cookies will stay fresh in an airtight container at room temperature for 2 days or in the refrigerator for up to 1 week.

SALLY SAYS

If your self-control is strong, wait until the next day to indulge. Like with banana bread, the flavor in these cookies is even more powerful and irresistible on day 2!

MAKE AHEAD-TIP

You can make the cookie dough through step 4 and chill it in an airtight container in the refrigerator for up to 4 days; before using, allow to come to room temperature, then continue with step 5. Baked cookies, without glaze, freeze well for up to 3 months; allow cookies to thaw overnight in the refrigerator, then bring to room temperature before glazing and serving.

WHOLE-WHEAT APPLE CINNAMON COOKIES

These nutty, cinnamon-spiced cookies are super soft and wholesome, and filled with sweet and juicy apples and plenty of chewy oats. The moisture in the apples keeps them extra tender, and to avoid an overly cakey cookie, make sure you gently blot the shredded apple in step 1. These cookies have the bonus of being relatively quick to make, too! The dough needs to chill for only 15 minutes.

PREP TIME: 15 minutes   **TOTAL TIME:** 1 hour 5 minutes   **YIELD:** 30 cookies

1 cup (150 g) shredded peeled apple
1½ cups (135 g) old-fashioned whole rolled oats
1 cup (120 g) whole-wheat flour
1 teaspoon baking soda
2 teaspoons ground cinnamon
½ teaspoon ground nutmeg
½ teaspoon salt
½ cup (1 stick, or 120 g) unsalted butter, softened to room temperature
½ cup (115 g) packed brown sugar
½ cup (100 g) granulated sugar
1 large egg, room temperature
1 teaspoon pure vanilla extract
2 tablespoons (30 ml) milk
¾ cup (90 g) chopped walnuts

MAKE-AHEAD TIP

See page 12.

1. Gently blot the shredded apple with a paper towel to remove some of the moisture. Set aside.

2. Whisk the oats, flour, baking soda, cinnamon, nutmeg, and salt together in a medium bowl. Set aside.

3. In a large bowl, using a handheld mixer or a stand mixer fitted with a paddle attachment, beat the butter on medium-high speed until smooth, about 1 minute. Add the brown sugar and granulated sugar, and beat on medium-high speed until creamed, about 2 minutes. Add the egg, vanilla extract, and milk, and beat on high speed until combined, about 1 minute. Scrape down the sides and up the bottom of the bowl and beat again as needed to combine.

4. Add the dry ingredients to the wet ingredients and mix on low speed until combined. With the mixer running on low speed, beat in the apple and walnuts. The dough will be thick and sticky. Cover and chill in the refrigerator for 15 minutes.

5. Preheat oven to 350°F (180°C). Line baking sheets with parchment paper or silicone baking mats. Set aside.

6. Scoop balls of dough, about 1½ tablespoons (No. 40 scoop) of dough per cookie, and place 3 inches (7.5 cm) apart on the baking sheets.

7. Bake for 12 to 13 minutes, or until lightly browned on the sides. The centers will look very soft.

8. Remove from the oven and allow the cookies to cool on the baking sheets for 5 minutes before transferring to a wire rack to cool completely.

9. Cookies will stay fresh in an airtight container at room temperature for up to 1 week.

Lemon Crème Sandwiches

Two buttery, flaky melt-in-your-mouth shortbread cookies with a hint of ginger and plenty of zippy lemon flavor enclose a lemon cream cheese frosting. These bright and cheery cookie sandwiches will channel summertime no matter the weather outside your window!

PREP TIME: 35 minutes   **TOTAL TIME:** 1 hour   **YIELD:** 30 cookie sandwiches

Cookies

1½ cups (3 sticks, or 360 g) unsalted butter, softened to room temperature

1 cup (120 g) confectioners' sugar

1 teaspoon pure vanilla extract

1 teaspoon lemon extract

2 teaspoons lemon zest

2¾ (330 g) cups all-purpose flour, plus more for work surface and rolling out

½ teaspoon salt

½ teaspoon ground ginger

Cream Cheese Frosting

4 ounces (227 g) block cream cheese, softened to room temperature

2 tablespoons (30 g) unsalted butter, softened to room temperature

2 cups (240 g) confectioners' sugar

1½ tablespoons (23 ml) fresh lemon juice

1. Preheat oven to 350°F (180°C). Line baking sheets with parchment paper or silicone baking mats. Set aside.

2. **To make the cookies:** In a large bowl, using a handheld mixer or a stand mixer fitted with a paddle attachment, beat the butter on medium-high speed until smooth, about 1 minute. Add confectioners' sugar, vanilla extract, lemon extract, and lemon zest, and beat on medium-high speed until combined and creamy, about 2 minutes. Scrape down the sides and up the bottom of the bowl and beat again as needed to combine.

3. Switch the mixer to low speed and slowly add the flour, ¼ cup (30 g) at a time. Once all of the flour is incorporated, add the salt and ginger. Turn the mixer up to high speed and beat until the dough comes together. Continue beating the dough until it becomes smooth.

4. Turn the dough out onto a lightly floured work surface. Divide into 2 equal portions. Roll one portion out to ¼ inch (6 mm) thickness. Using a 2-inch (5 cm) round cookie cutter, cut into circles. Reroll the remaining dough and continue cutting until all is used. Repeat with the second portion. You should have about 60 circles.

5. Place the cookies 3 inches (7.5 cm) apart on the baking sheets and lightly prick the top of each with a fork. (The latter is only for looks and can be skipped!) Bake until very lightly browned on the edges, 12 to 14 minutes.

6. Remove from the oven and allow to cool on the baking sheets for 5 minutes before transferring to a wire rack to cool completely.

7. **To make the frosting:** In a medium bowl, using a handheld mixer or a stand mixer fitted with a whisk attachment, beat the cream cheese and butter together on medium-high speed until completely smooth. Add the confectioners' sugar and lemon juice, and beat on low speed for 20 seconds, then increase to high speed until combined, about 1 minute.

8. Spread about ¾ teaspoon of frosting on half of the cooled cookies. Carefully top each with another cookie to create a sandwich.

9. Cookies will stay fresh in an airtight container at room temperature for 1 day or in the refrigerator for up to 1 week.

MAKE AHEAD-TIP

You can prepare the cookie dough and chill it in an airtight container in the refrigerator for up to 3 days; before using, allow to come to room temperature, then continue with step 4. Another option is to freeze the dough for up to 3 months; thaw overnight in the refrigerator and then bring to room temperature before continuing with step 4. Baked cookies, without frosting, freeze well for up to 3 months; thaw overnight in the refrigerator and, if desired, bring to room temperature before frosting and serving.

Toasted S'more Cookie Cups

I can't write a cookie cookbook without including one of the best flavor combinations on the planet: S'MORES! Here we're switching things up and baking s'mores into cookie cups. The cookie cups are flavored with graham crackers, topped with an ooey-gooey toasted marshmallow, and finished off with a piece of milk chocolate. Best part of all? No campfire required!

PREP TIME: 20 minutes   **TOTAL TIME:** 1 hour 30 minutes   **YIELD:** 32 cookies

1¼ cups (170 g) all-purpose flour
1 cup (85 g) graham cracker crumbs
 (about 7 full sheets of graham
 crackers, ground up)
½ teaspoon baking soda
½ teaspoon salt
¾ cup (1½ sticks, or 180 g) unsalted
 butter, softened to room temperature
¾ cup (170 g) packed brown sugar
¼ cup (50 g) granulated sugar
1 large egg, room temperature
1 teaspoon pure vanilla extract
16 marshmallows, sliced in half
32 milk chocolate bar pieces

MAKE AHEAD-TIP

Prepare the cookie dough through step 4. Cover and chill the dough in the refrigerator for at least 1 hour and up to 4 days before continuing with step 5.

1. Preheat oven to 350°F (180°C). Generously grease a 24-count mini-muffin pan or spray with nonstick spray. You will need to make a second batch or use another 24-count mini-muffin pan since this recipe makes 32 cookies.

2. Whisk the flour, graham cracker crumbs, baking soda, and salt together in a medium bowl. Set aside.

3. In a large bowl, using a handheld mixer or a stand mixer fitted with a paddle attachment, beat the butter on medium-high speed until smooth, about 1 minute. Add the brown sugar and granulated sugar, and beat on medium-high speed until creamed, about 2 minutes. Add the egg and vanilla extract, and beat on high speed until combined, about 1 minute. Scrape down the sides and up the bottom of the bowl and beat again as needed to combine.

4. Add the dry ingredients to the wet ingredients and mix on low speed until combined.

5. Roll balls of dough, using 1 tablespoon of dough per cookie. Place each dough ball into its own pan cup. Bake for 18 to 20 minutes, or until cookies appear set on the sides.

6. Remove from the oven and allow to cool for 10 minutes before removing the cookie cups from the muffin pan(s). Switch oven to broil mode. Transfer cookie cups to a baking sheet, then top each with a marshmallow half.

7. Broil for 1 minute so the marshmallows can toast. Watch closely to make sure the marshmallows do not burn. Immediately remove from the oven once the marshmallows are lightly toasted.

8. Press a chocolate bar piece into each warm marshmallow. Allow to cool for 10 minutes before enjoying warm, or let cool completely.

9. Cookie cups are best enjoyed the day they are made, as the marshmallows don't hold up well much longer after that.

Espresso White Chocolate Chunk Cookies

I'm all about pairing cookies with a hot cup o' joe in the afternoon, but what about adding that coffee flavor directly to the cookie dough? We explored this with Coffee Toffee Shortbread (page 93), but let's kick up the espresso a couple of notches and add some sweet white chocolate to smooth out its flavor. You know I have to say it: have your coffee and eat it, too!

PREP TIME: 30 minutes   **TOTAL TIME:** 2 hours 30 minutes   **YIELD:** 36 cookies

2½ cups (300 g) all-purpose flour

4 teaspoons (8 g) espresso powder

1 teaspoon baking soda

½ teaspoon salt

1 cup (2 sticks, or 240 g) unsalted butter, softened to room temperature

1 cup (225 g) packed brown sugar

½ cup (100 g) granulated sugar

2 large eggs, room temperature

2 teaspoons pure vanilla extract

2 (4 ounces, or 113 g, each) bars white chocolate, coarsely chopped

2 tablespoons (20 g) white chocolate chips (optional)

MAKE-AHEAD TIP

See page 12.

Sally Says

Don't confuse espresso powder with ground coffee. Espresso powder (aka instant espresso) is super concentrated, highly flavorful, and dissolves quickly with liquid. Pick up a jar to use with this book and try adding a teaspoon or 2 to brownies, chocolate cakes, and cupcakes.

1. Whisk the flour, espresso powder, baking soda, and salt together in a medium bowl. Set aside.

2. In a large bowl, using a handheld mixer or a stand mixer fitted with a paddle attachment, beat the butter on medium-high speed until smooth, about 1 minute. Add the brown sugar and granulated sugar, and beat on medium-high speed until creamed, about 2 minutes. Add the eggs and vanilla extract, and beat on high speed until combined, about 1 minute. Scrape down the sides and up the bottom of the bowl and beat again as needed to combine.

3. Add the dry ingredients to the wet ingredients and mix on low speed until combined. With the mixer running on low speed, add the chopped white chocolate. The dough will be soft and thick. Cover and chill the dough in the refrigerator for at least 1½ hours (and up to 4 days). If chilling for longer than 3 hours, allow it to sit at room temperature for at least 30 minutes before rolling and baking because the dough will be quite hard.

4. Preheat oven to 350°F (180°C). Line baking sheets with parchment paper or silicone baking mats. Set aside.

5. Roll balls of dough, about 1½ tablespoons of dough per cookie, and place 3 inches (7.5 cm) apart on the baking sheets. Bake for 12 to 13 minutes, or until lightly browned on the sides. The centers will look very soft.

6. Remove from the oven and allow to cool on the baking sheets for 5 minutes before transferring to a wire rack to cool completely. While the cookies are still warm, press a few white chocolate chips (if desired) into the top of each.

7. Cookies will stay fresh in an airtight container at room temperature for up to 1 week.

INDEX

ACKNOWLEDGMENTS

This cookbook came to life in my kitchen, but I wasn't the only person behind the craft. Thank you to the entire Race Point Publishing crew for helping me author my favorite cookbook yet. Many thanks especially to Jeannine Dillon, Erin Canning, Merideth Harte, Jacqui Caulton, Mary Aarons, and Steven Pomije.

I have so much gratitude for my supportive and loving cheerleaders—my dear family and friends who have taste-tested so many of these cookie creations. I know it was a difficult job, but someone had to do it! Thank you especially to my mom and dad and parents-in-law for your endless encouragement through this writing process and the course of my entire unpredictable career.

Thank you to my assistants, Steph and Hilari. You help me maintain my sanity each day, and you kept my business running throughout the creation of this manuscript. And thank you for joining me in the kitchen for several recipes in this book, Steph!

Thank you to my husband, Kevin, without whose never-ending love and encouragement, this book wouldn't be in anyone's hands today. Thank you, Kevin, for helping with the daily cookie-baking marathons, doing all the dishes (all the time, every day), running to the grocery store a minimum of 15 times per week, and for reminding me to take time for myself. And for doing all of this with a smile. And, most importantly, thank you for believing in me during the times I didn't.

One of the best parts of writing a food blog is that I get to hear directly from readers from all over the world. Thank you to the *Sally's Baking Addiction* community of readers whose excitement for this cookbook kept me churning out content. You shared your favorite cookies, which helped me create the Contents for this very book. You guys have a cookie addiction, too, and you just GET me. We're baking soulmates, you and me. I love you all!